STUDIES IN THE HISTORY O
VOLUME

CW00392163

IN THE Sv. ...

THE ORIGINS AND SYSTEMATIC DEVELOPMENT OF SWIMMING IN THE COUNTY OF SURREY'S PUBLIC ELEMENTARY SCHOOLS 1905-1921
PIONEERED BY MAJOR ARTHUR ORMAND NORMAN
A DOCUMENTARY HISTORY
WITH VARIOUS APPENDICES
INCLUDING
SWIMMING AND WASHING VERMINOUS CHILDREN IN THE LONDON SCHOOL BOARD

by

J Robert Pegg
MA (Ed) History of Education (1870-1939)
MA (Ed) Curriculum Studies
Chairman, Ealing Primary Schools' Athletic Association 1996-2003
and Ealing Primary Schools' Football Association 1998-2003

abpublishing
Ripley, Surrey

Published by
Angela Blaydon Publishing Ltd
2 Elm Close, Ripley, GU23 6LE
www.abpublishing.com

ISBN: 978-0-9539821-8-9

Cover design and typesetting
© Angela Blaydon Publishing Ltd

Cover images
Front Cover: 'To swim like a dog' p.164
Back Cover: 'To swim with one hand and one foot upon his back' p.176
both images taken from *De Arte Natandi Libriduo, quorum Prior regulas ipsius artis, posterior verò praxin
demonstrationemque continet* by Everard Digby, London, Excudebat Thomas Dawson, 1587 (EEBO Edition held in
the Boston Library)

Set in Times 10pt
Printed on paper from sustainable sources

Printed by Hobbs the Printers Ltd, Totton, Hants. SO40 3WX
www.hobbs.uk.com

CONTENTS

LIST OF ILLUSTRATIONS

ACKNOWLEDGEMENTS

My grateful thanks to the staff of the Surrey History Centre (SHC) in Woking for their help in making this book possible.

My thanks also to Mrs Evelyn Cowie who supervised my dissertation on *The Impact of Contemporary and Historical Influences on Aspects of Physical Education in Elementary Schools in Surrey 1894-1930* as part fulfilment of the requirements for the degree of Master of Arts (Education) at King's College, University of London in 1985. This book represents an extension of the ideas and the research expressed in that dissertation.

Many thanks also to Christopher Nixon for his expertise in IT and online Investigations.
Many thanks to the Surrey History Centre for permission to reproduce

(1) Charlie Warner Medallists 1897-1938(Appendix III)

(2) Programme for the 7th Annual Swimming Sports 21 September 1904 (Appendix IV)

(3) Girls' Championship Medallists 1908-1938 (Appendix V)

OTHER BOOKS BY THE AUTHOR

This book is one of a series of three dealing with the educational history of the Surrey Educational Committee between the Education Acts of 1902 and 1921.

"In Sickness and in Health" The Origins and Systematic Development of Children's Medical Inspection and Treatment in Surrey's Public Elementary Schools 1905-1921 Pioneered by Dr Thomas Henry Jones: A Documentary History.

"Stand at Ease" The Origins and Systematic Development of Children's Physical Training in the County of Surrey's Public Elementary Schools 1905-1921 Pioneered by Major Arthur Ormand Norman: A Documentary History.

~~~~~~~~~~~

Other Books

Quick March! to Athletic Sports: The Origins and Development of Drill, Athletics, Cricket, Football and Swimming in Croydon's Public Elementary Schools 1893-1910: A Newspaper, Documentary History.

ABBREVIATIONS

1870 Act	Elementary Education Act 1870
1873 Act	Elementary Education Act 1873
1890 Report	School Board for London: Report of the Physical Education Sub-Committee Bathing and Swimming Classes with (Sub) Appendices
1902 Act	The Education Act, 1902 2 EDW 7 chapter 42
1904 Report	Report of the Inter-Departmental Committee on Physical Deterioration
1904 Syllabus	Syllabus of Physical Exercises for use in Public Elementary Schools, 1904
AD	Anno Domini
ASA	Amateur Swimming Association
Board	Board of Education (Board of Education Act, 1899. 62 and 63 Victoria chapter 33.)
Ch. Ch.	Christ Church
C of E	Church of England
circular 515	Circular 515 dated 26 August 1904
code	Code of Regulations for Day Schools with Schedules and Appendices
Cross Commission	Reports of The Royal Commission to enquire Into the working of the Elementary Education Acts, 1886-1888
Education Department	Committee of the Privy Council on Education
Hansard	Parliamentary Debates
HMI	Her/His Majesty's Inspector
i.e. (id est)	that is
KBE	Knight Commander of the Order of the British Empire
LCC	London County Council
Lea	Local Education Authority
LGB	Local Government Board
LLD	Doctor of Laws
LSSA	London Schools Swimming Association
MI	Medical Inspection
MIPTS	Medical Inspection & Physical Training Sub-committee
MO	Medical Officer
Model Course	A Model Course of Physical Training for Use in the Upper Departments of Public Elementary Schools, 1902 Circular 452, 20 June 1901
MP	Member of Parliament
nd	no date

NP	No page
OUP	Oxford University Press
PE	Physical Education
PES	Public Elementary Schools
PT	Physical Training
RC	Roman Catholic
RLSS	Royal Life Saving Society
SC	Swimming Club
SCC	Surrey County Council
SEC	Surrey Education Committee
SHC	Surrey History Centre
SMO	School Medical Officer
Special Committee Cognate	Special Committee on Physical Training & Medical Inspection
St	Saint
TNA	The National Archives
UDC	Urban District Council

Bathing & Swimming —

Plate I.   Illustration A. Swimming as portrayed in *Gymnastics For Youth*, 1800 (Plate 10 referring to page 339 the beginning of Chapter X on Swimming) (*see* Note 26 Introduction)

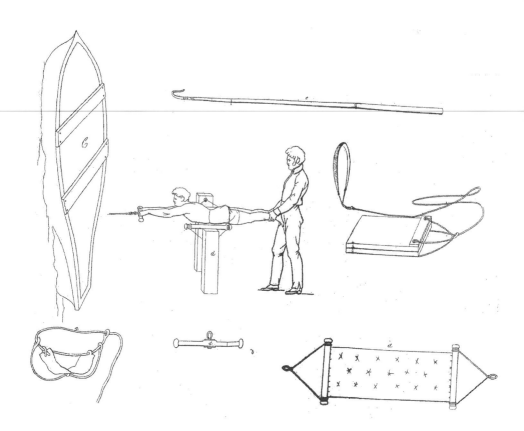

Plate II.   Illustration B. Swimming Aids presented in Plate 7 of *An Elementary Course of Gymnastic Exercises*, 1825 (*see* Note 30 Introduction)

Plate III. Illustration C. Edited diagrams from Plate 8 (Figs 4, 5 and 6 noted on page 166; fig 11 on page 174; fig. 13 on page 177); Plate 9 (fig. 9 on page 171) of *An Elementary Course of Gymnastic Exercises*, 1825 (*see* Note 30 Introduction)

HOWARD'S METHOD.—HOW TO RESTORE THE DROWNED.

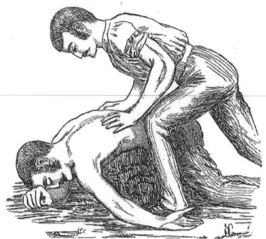

FIG. 14.—PRESSING AND DRAINING WATER FROM
LUNGS AND STOMACH.

1. *Instantly* turn the patient downwards, with a large firm roll of clothing under stomach and chest.

2. Place one of his arms under his forehead, so as to keep his mouth off the ground.

3. Press with all your weight two or three times, for four or five seconds each time, upon the patient's back, so that the water may be pressed out of lungs and stomach, and drain freely out of the mouth.

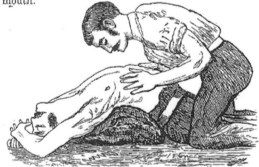

FIG. 15.—THE BELLOWS-BLOWING MOVEMENT, FOR PRESSING FOUL
AIR OUT AND DRAWING PURE AIR INTO THE LUNGS.

P

Plate IV. Illustration D. Howard's Method of Life Saving in *Health At School*, 1887 (*see* Note 31 Introduction)

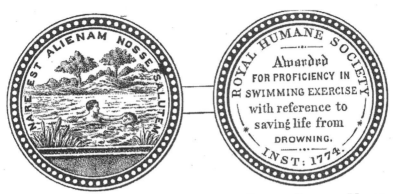

FIG. 21.—THE ROYAL HUMANE SOCIETY PUBLIC SCHOOLS MEDAL.

ROYAL HUMANE SOCIETY.

INSTITUTED 1774.

SUPPORTED BY VOLUNTARY CONTRIBUTIONS.

PATRON,
HER MAJESTY THE QUEEN.

VICE PATRONS,
H.R.H. THE DUKE OF YORK, K.G., &c.
H.R.H. THE DUKE OF CAMBRIDGE, K.G., G.C.M.G.

PRESIDENT,
HIS GRACE THE DUKE OF ARGYLL, K.G., K.T.

This is to Certify that a Silver Medallion for "Proficiency in Swimming Exercises with reference to saving Life from Drowning" has been awarded to

_____

_____

_____

SECRETARY.   CHAIRMAN.

4, *Trafalgar Square,*
London, W.C.

Z

Plate V. Illustration E. The Royal Humane Society Public School Medal as portrayed in *Health At School,* 1894 (*see* Note 31 Introduction)

INTRODUCTION

There are some brief references to swimming in Plato's: *The Republic*[1], *The Laws*[2] and *Phaedrus*[3]. In *Schools Of Hellas*, 1922[4], there are various references to swimming. In *Early British Swimming 55BC-AD1719*, 1983[5], Nicholas Orme gives an extensive account of swimming with fully referenced notes. He also includes a full English translation of the first English treatise on swimming with diagrams by Christopher Middleton,[6] while the Latin version, *De Arte Natandi*, 1595,[7] from which it is translated is also available complete with diagrams. Some of these diagrams are also included in *Hung Out To Dry*, 2011[8], and *The Story of Swimming*, 2011[9], both of which are social histories, the latter, in particular quoting lines from the Anglo-Saxon Poem, *Beowulf*,[10] and noting other treatises on cold-water swimming.[11]

Beowulf was not the only poem of "splendour and artistry; an eloquent celebration of a heroic life and death; an 'action' of epic sweep and scope."[12]

The legend of Horatius Cocles reputed to have defended the Pons Sublicius, which led across the River Tiber towards Rome, against the Etruscans led by Lars Porsena has several versions. No one knows what the true version is, or, even, whether or not the story was based on fact. The version below, is that of Lord Macauley's *Lays of Ancient Rome*, 1842,[13] which was an attempt to reconstruct legendary Roman history in the form of the poetic ballad. The verses quoted below are those selected for their reference to swimming.

Verse LVIX

"Oh, Tiber! Father Tiber!
To whom the Romans pray
A Roman's life, a Roman's arms
Take thou in charge this day!"
So he spake, and speaking sheathed
The good sword by his side,
And with his harness on his back,
Plunged headlong in the tide.

LX

No sound of joy or sorrow
Was heard from either bank:
But friends and foes in dumb surprise,
With parted lips and straining eyes,
Stood gazing where he sank;
And when above the surges,
They saw his crest appear,
All Rome sent forth a rapturous cry,

And even the ranks of Tuscany
Could scarce forbear to cheer.

LXI

But fiercely ran the current,
Swollen high by months of rain:
And fast his blood was flowing;
And he was sore in pain,
And heavy with his armour,
And spent with changing blows:
And oft they thought him sinking,
But still again he rose.

LXII

Never, I ween, did swimmer,
In such an evil case,
Struggle through such a raging flood
Safe to the landing place:
But his limbs were borne up bravely
By the brave heart within,
And our good father Tiber
Bare bravely up his chin.

LXIII

"Curse on him!" quoth false Sextus;
"Will not the villain drown?
But for this stay, ere close of day
We should have sacked the town!"
"Heaven help him!" quoth Lars Porsena
"And bring him safe to shore;
For such a gallant feat of arms
Was never seen before."

LXIV

And now he feels the bottom;
Now on dry earth he stands;
Now round him throng the Fathers;
To press his gory hands;
And now, with shouts and clapping,
And noise of weeping loud,
He enters through the River-Gate
Borne by the joyous crowd.

In *The Compleat Gentleman*, 1634, Henry Peacham (1576-1643) recounted the story in the following way:[14]

"The skill and art of swimming is also very requisite in every Noble and Gentleman, especially if he looks for employment in the wars, for hereby (besides the preserving of his own life upon infinite occasions,) he may many ways annoy his enemy. Horatius Cocles only by the benefit of swimming saved his country, for when himself alone had long defended and made good the bridge over (the) Tiber against the Etruscans, the Romans broke it down behind him, where with, in his Armour he cast himself into the river, and (notwithstanding a shower of Darts and Arrows were sent after him) swam with safety into the city, which rewarded him with a Statue erected in the Market Place, and as much land as he could encompass with a plough in a day."

(Please note the English has been updated)

Swimming had achieved a kind of legendary status long before that of Horatius, however, with the story of Hero and Leander recounted in brief by Richard Mulcaster (*ca* 1530-1611) in *Positions*, 1561.[15] It was the nature of the story that prompted Mulcaster to note that the considerations of their affair might recommend swimming also.

The Hellespont was the narrow channel between the Sea of Mamara and the Aegean Sea. There was, therefore, two sides; the Asian side and the European side. Leander lived on the Asian side but fell in love with Hero living on the European side. True love was thwarted by the geography of their respective positions. Not only that, but the Hellespont was renowned as problematical to navigate. Furthermore, their relationship was strained in the personal sense that Hero was a priestess of Aphrodite and sworn to everlasting celibacy. Undeterred, the couple met at night with Leander swimming the Hellespont in order to gain access to Hero's charms. On one occasion Leander lost control of his destination and was swept out into the Aegean Sea. Hero was so devastated, that, by way of throwing herself into the Hellespont, she joined her lover.

Christopher Marlowe (1564-1593) also related the story[16] part of which proceeds:

"O Hero, Hero!" thus he cried full oft;
And then he got him to a rock aloft,
Where having spied her tower, long stared he on't,
And prayed the narrow toiling Hellespont
To part in twain, that he might come and go;
But still the rising billows answered "No"
With that he stripped him to the ivory skin
And, crying "Love, I come," leaped lively in.
Whereat the sapphire visaged god grew proud,
And made his capering Triton sound aloud,
Imagining that Ganymede, displeased,
Had left the heavens; therefore on him he seized.
Leander strived; the waves about him wound,
And pulled him to the bottom, where the ground
Was strewed with pearl, and low in coral groves
Sweet singing mermaids sported with their loves

On heaps of heavy gold, and took great pleasure
To spurn in careless sort the shipwrack treasure

Leander, being up, began to swim
And looking back, saw Neptune follow him
Whereat aghast, the poor soul 'gan to cry
"O, let me visit Hero ere I die!"
The god put Helle's bracelet on his arm,
And swore the sea should never do him harm.

The poem gave a warning, therefore, to avoid swimming in certain kinds of water, which was reflected by other writers.[17] Swimming in hot water springs was good for the palsy and the use of swimming aids was virtuously beneficial. It was also reasonable to swim in lakes and meres where the water was clear. Nevertheless, it was wise not to swim too long in fresh water for fear of perishing the sinews with cold and moisture which caused the cramp and was a danger to swimmers. There was an obvious peril in water but fresh river water was a healthy place to swim and was good preparation for sleep. Even so, salt water was the best in which to swim because it afforded buoyancy to the swimmer and was, therefore, conducive to less effort being expended. It was also good for removing headaches, freeing stuffed nostrils and thus helped to make possible the nose to smell better. It was also good for dropsy, scabs, scurvy, smallpox, leprosy and "falling away of either leg" or any other part and a host of other complaints. Swimming, however, was good for children to learn since it helped in saving them from private danger. Moreover, if in the country's defence he/she died on land he/she had done his/her duty, yet, if he/she were to be drowned in defending the country, then he/she had not done his/her duty.[18]

John Locke (1632-1704) in *Some Thoughts Concerning Education*, 1693[19], refers to a Roman ideal that swimming ought to be ranked with the learning of letters, although, in the Athens tradition of Greek education, every boy had to be proficient in reading, writing and swimming in order to be considered educated.[20] As well as being a skill which was useful at at time of need it was advantageous to health if one bathed in cold water in the heat of summer.[21]

Jean-Jacques Rousseau (1712-1778) published *Emile* in 1762. This book was the beginning of modern educational reform with the child as the centre of the educational process. The young Emile would spend most of his time out of doors, running about, scarcely clothed, leading a vigorous, free and natural life. Exercise the body of the child, his limbs, his senses his strength but his mind should be kept idle as long as possible.[22]

Moreover, *Emile*

"should be as much at home in the water as on the land. Why should he not be able to live in every element? .....People are afraid lest the child should be drowned while he is learning to swim; if he dies while he is learning, or if he dies because he has not learnt, it will be your own fault......As the exercise does not depend on its danger, he will learn to swim the *Hellespont* (my italics) by swimming, without any danger, a stream in his father's park;"[23]

Placing so much emphasis on physical education (PE) was not redressing the balance of *mens sana in corpore sano*,[24] it was rather that Rousseau was following the ideas of John

Locke that all knowledge was acquired through the senses, rejecting the ideas of Rene Descartes (1596-1650) that knowledge was innately gained by the reproductive process.[25]

Nevertheless, a sound mind in a strong and healthy body had for ages been the grand object of education,[26] was the mantra that Johann Christoph Friedrich Guts Muths (1759-1839) expounded in Gymnastics for Youth, 1800. The chapter on swimming covers twenty-two pages[27] and a range of differing aspects of swimming including the fact that the cold bath is conducive to health and cleanliness and is an essential object of good physical education. A bathing place was indispensable (see Illustration A) and for those parents concerned about colds, coughs and other diseases from bathing in cold water, Guts Muths offered the assurance that he had pursued the habit of bathing in about thirty young people throughout all the seasons. The best place to exercise the body was the neighbouring river gentle in current, deep enough for diving and screened by bushes. Ponds were unsuitable.

Guts Muths expresses seven simple rules for the initial training of young people including a summer bathe in the afternoon when the water had warmed; on no account after a meal; that they take to the water while cool; to jump into the water instantaneously covering the whole body, or, for the non-exuberant, to enter the water dipping one's head gradually; five or ten minutes was enough to strengthen the nerves and refresh the body which should then be rubbed down; there should be no restraint from bathing even though they may have the temporary affliction of a cold or cough and should make haste in drying themselves off as soon as possible after leaving the water.

In many respects these initial bathing techniques were a prelude to the art of swimming since one learned to familiarise oneself with the buoyancy of the water. Secondly, if the water reached the hips it was deep enough for swimming. Thirdly, an assistant in the water was very useful, even if he couldn't swim, because, if he placed his hand on the belly, the swimmer gained encouragement from not being able to sink. Fourthly, having gained confidence from the assistant's help he should be further helped by a belt passing round the body at the armpits and controlled by the assistant with a cord at a depth in which the swimmer was up to his neck. Fifthly, in projecting the body, belly facing downwards towards the bottom of the river, the chin should be above the water but the hands and feet should not rise up above the surface. The resulting explanation seems to be that which is consistent with the present-day notion of the breast stroke, although McIntosh suggests that it wasn't until 1809 that the breast stroke was first developed.[28] Sixthly, in the back stroke, one should have only the face above the water with the hands and knees being drawn up in order to propel one along the surface of the water, a sort of breast stroke in reverse. Moreover, this stroke was very handy if one became tired since one could rest the legs but keep oneself afloat by short movement strokes of the hands. If one sustained cramp while swimming on the back, one should raise the offending leg out of the water and give it a sudden, vigorous and violent jerk in the air. Treading water was also another method of resting when tired.[29]

In spite of Guts Muths commitment to swimming the main basis of his book was devoted to physical exercises which included athletic, dancing and gymnastic activities. A similar treatise was first published in 1823,[30] which went to a fourth edition entitled *An Elementary Course of Gymnastic Exercises Intended to Develop and Improve the Physical Powers of Man with the Report Made to the Medical Faculty of Paris on the Subject and a New and Complete Treatise on the Art of Swimming*, 1825, written by P H Clias. The book contains three plates (7, 8 and 9) on swimming but it is difficult to marry up the text with the diagrams in Plates 8 and 9 as it is not always clear from the text which diagrams refer exactly to the text. For that reason not all the diagrams are shown in Illustration C, but, those that are,

are shown as a small compendium, without prejudice to the text which may be found in Chapter IV, a total of thirty-six pages. Illustration B refers exclusively to Plate 7.

In *Health At School*, 1887, Clement Dukes of Rugby School refers to the use of a river for summer bathing.[31] It was preferable to have a swimming bath under cover that could be heated all year round and whose size could be regulated by the number of boys in the school. The temperature should never fall below 65°F or be above 70°F. Naturally these conditions were conducive to the health of the children. Dukes had some important rules for bathers devised by the "Royal Humane Society"

"(1)   Time of bathing - If bathing is to be a source of health
   1.   Avoid bathing within 2 hours after a meal.
   2.   Avoid bathing when exhausted by fatigue or any other cause
   3.   Avoid bathing when the body is cooling after perspiration
   4.   Avoid bathing altogether in the open-air if, after having been a short time in the water, there is a sense of chilliness with numbness of the hands and feet; but
   5.   Bathe when the body is warm, provided no time is lost in getting into the water
   6.   Avoid chilling the body by sitting or standing UNDRESSED on the banks or in boats after having been in the water.
   7.   Avoid remaining too long in the water; leave the water immediately there is the slightest feeling of chilliness.
   8.   The vigorous and young may bathe early in the morning on an empty stomach
   9.   The young, and those who are weak, had better bathe two or three after a meal; the best time for such is from two to three hours after breakfast.
   10. Those who are subject to attacks of giddiness or faintness, and those who suffer from palpitation and other sense of discomfort at the heart, should not bathe without first consulting their medical adviser.
   And I (Dukes) would add
   11. Bathe as many times a day as you like, provided you are not in the water for more than a few moments. In summer, a plunge and out again, several times a day, is not only refreshing but very invigorating.
(2)   Time in the water – The time boys are in the water should be measured in minutes and not in quarters of an hour. Bathing makes the skin more healthy but not prolonged bathing which has a depressing action on the skin and on the internal organs.
(3)   Life Saving by Swimming – In the year 1882 he wrote to the "Royal Humane Society" about how to save a drowning person and proposing a competition between all the Public Schools which would be rewarded with a silver medal for saving life from drowning. The "Royal Humane Society" responded with the award of a silver medal (Illustration E) for each great Public School *for the best practice in rescue from drowning*."

Dukes then relates the rules to be observed in the competition.[32] Dukes, however, was not just satisfied with a return to land but was, himself, to award a silver challenge cup for the best practice in the restoration of the *apparently drowned* when he had been brought to land, presumed dead, unless immediate help be at hand. It was important for the boys to realise that they might not have time to wait for medical help; therefore, Dukes had taught the boys *Howards' Method* (Illustration D), which could be carried out by one boy and was simple and efficacious to implement.[33]

The first reference to school baths in the Sheffield School Board was in February 1881 when it was decided that the architects should consider on the best method of providing a bath or baths at the Duchess Road Schools,[34] which came to nothing. This disappointment was overcome by a resolution of the Sheffield Town Council, dated 7 April 1881, which proposed that children of the Board Schools be allowed to use the Corporation Baths on certain days at a charge of a ha'penny a head between the hours of 7:30 and 9:30am provided the children were accompanied by a teacher or other competent person. Consequently the Corporation and Attercliffe Baths were used, four mornings a week in each case. Ten of the boys' schools within easy reach of these facilities were catered for.

Nevertheless, this scheme seems to have fallen into disrepute but in February 1897 the School Management Committee sanctioned an experiment to introduce swimming into the physical exercises for the children attending Attercliffe Boys' Elementary School. Attendance was free on Friday afternoons for the boys of the school only.

This concession was apparently extended to a wider group of children in the elementary schools during school hours on Tuesdays, Wednesdays and Fridays and a charge of a ha'penny and a penny was made at other times by privilege tickets. Girls were also admitted at the Glossop Road Ladies' Bath.

At a further meeting of the School Management Committee in November 1902 embracing new regulations for free admission and the award of certificates for children who learned to swim. The meeting also suggested the formation of swimming clubs for male and female teachers and by the appointment of an Instructor in swimming, which apparently did not reach fruition.[35]

The question of swimming instruction during school hours, after 1902, seems to have been a particularly fraught one especially if it was free. The first factor seems to have been the problem of what constituted an "Attendance":

> "Swimming, *if appearing on the time table*, and cricket, "if carried on under proper supervision for instruction in the rules of the game, and in the art of preserving a good temper," may count towards "attendances."[36] (*author's italics*)

As late as September 1908, for instance, the Board of Education (Board) addressed at some length a problem reported by the Inspector of two schools, Burley-in-Wharfedale Main Street Council School and Burley-in-Wharfedale Church of England (C of E) School who travelled to Ilkley by train in order to have swimming lessons.[37] The Board were made aware that it had been the practice for the children attending swimming lessons to leave school about 1:45pm and not return to school after the swimming lesson. Since the schools met from 1:30pm to 4pm practically the whole of the afternoon was occupied by the swimming lesson and by travelling to and from Ilkley. The Board were prepared to allow a reasonable time spent on going to and from swimming baths to be included for purposes of the grant under Article 43 (b) of the *Code of Day Regulations* (code), but it did not regard the time spent in that case to be reasonable. It appeared to the Board very doubtful whether the attendances of the children in question should have been counted for Grant purposes.

In reply to a letter from the Board, the Local Education Authority (Lea) concerning Burley-in-Wharfedale Main Street Council School (Council Schools were Elementary Schools) replied that the baths were three miles from Burley. It was necessary for the children to travel by train. The Lea were endeavouring to arrange the swimming lessons to take place in the mornings, which would obviate the need for the head teacher to travel with the boys, as before, and, therefore, not leave the school in a state of disorganisation. The situation was apparently resolved on this basis but the Inspector was to report on the new regime's practical working.[38]

The second factor was that "of the requirements of the code". In 1904, for example, the Borough of Newark Education Committee wrote to the Board asking whether or not they could donate to the Newark Swimming Association.[39] A large number of children of both sexes had for years received free tuition from the Association without charge. Swimming was not included in any of the school curricula. The Board replied that any expenditure would be, in the first instance, a matter for the District Auditor. The Board, however, noted it would have no objection to the Lea making provision for instruction in swimming out of school hours provided that such instruction was not counted as school attendance under Article 12 of the code.[40] Even so, this was a complicated picture, one in which Robert Laurie Morant (1863-1920), permanent secretary at the Board felt compelled to write a note to repudiate that interpretation of the 1904 code,[41] quoting the last three lines of Section 7(1)(a) of The Education Act, 1902, (1902 Act). In effect, the Local Government Board (LGB) had intervened to deny the authority of Newark Lea to make a donation or annual subscription to the Newark Swimming Association in the circumstances described in the letter to the Board of which the Board had forwarded a copy to the LGB.[42]

A similar letter from the County Borough of Hastings appeared at the Board's offices in November 1904.[43] Once again the reply indicated that the legality of any expenditure was a matter for the District Auditor but with the further proviso of an appeal to the LGB. However, if an arrangement for the instruction of children in swimming on or two evenings a week were approved by His/Her Majesty's Inspector (HMI) and shown on the timetable of the schools affected, such instruction would be recognised by the Board as part of the school curriculum under Article 44(1) of the code, since the time so fixed on the timetable for instruction in swimming would form part of the school curriculum* and any expense in respect of it would properly be included in the expenditure required for maintaining the school. Morant had inserted curriculum*, rather than attendance, as the local bye-laws might conceivably have been worded as not to make attendance at evening swimming classes *compulsory*.[44]

A further letter concerned the appointment of a swimming instructor. Would such an appointment, asked the Cornwall Education Committee, form part of an approved system of Physical Exercises according to the requirements of the code for 1904? The Board took the view that instruction in swimming could not be considered as part of an approved system of Physical Exercises under Article 1(8) of the code. Swimming under a proper instructor might be taught as part of the *approved* (*author's italics*) curriculum, but, that its teaching, was exclusive of the minimum time required by Circular 515 (circular 515) dated 26 August 1904 for formal lessons in physical training (PT). The Board wished to encourage swimming but not to the exclusion of a due amount of other kinds of physical exercise,[45] to which the Cornwall Education Committee sent a protest against its, the Board's, refusal to recognise swimming as part of an approved course of physical exercise. (*The Schoolmaster*, 20 January 1906, page 118)

It would appear, therefore, that three factors were responsible for the partial interregnum of swimming in the period from 1902 to 1907. First, there had to be an approved system of swimming instruction by the HMI and the Board, which had to be entered on the timetable of the school particularly if this exceeded the normal hours of instruction of the school's day.

Secondly, an Lea could not authorise payments to a Schools' Swimming Association unless a bye-law existed to authorise such a payment, otherwise there would be repercussions from the LGB and the District Auditor. Thirdly, the Board could not authorise swimming as an alternative to the *Syllabus of Physical Exercises for use in Public Elementary Schools*, 1904 (1904 Syllabus), which had been included with circular 515, and had come about as a result of the *Report of the Inter-Departmental Committee on Physical Deterioration*, 1904 (1904 Report), which itself had been established as a result of perceived Boer War deficiencies in the physical prowess of British Army recruits.

The first Public Elementary School (PES) swimming pool was opened at the Wapping Road school in Bradford in 1898 at roughly the same time as London was contemplating a similar development.[46] Wapping Road was one of twelve "Public Baths" listed in *The Complete Swimmer*, 1912,[47] which existed in Bradford. The credit for the establishment of school swimming baths in Bradford, of which there were six in 1924, was credited to Margaret McMillan in *Crowley's Hygiene of School Life*, 1924. Nevertheless, they were used as centres for adjacent schools.[48]

The circumstances of Surrey's Elementary Schools were considerably different in that respect. In all of the Reports[49] of the development of swimming in Surrey's Elementary Schools there were, of course, public baths in some of the larger towns such as Dorking but essentially Surrey, in the early 20th century, was a county of a largely rural character.

Swimming took place in a variety of places, such as rivers, ponds, private bathing places and public swimming baths (*see* Appendices XI-XVI).

Problematically, little is said of the strokes that children were taught, although there are references to the use of occasional swimming aids ordered by the Superintendent of Physical Training during the course of his attempts to engage schools in a curriculum of swimming. Despite the interruption of the First World War, the developments recounted in the following pages trace the course of change from 1907 to 1921 in Surrey's PES.

Notes

1. Plato (Lee, HDF, translated). *The Republic*, 207, paragraph 453, Penguin Books Ltd., Harmondsworth, Middlesex, 1955.

2. Plato (Saunders, Trevor J translated). *The Laws*, 137, paragraph 689, Penguin Books Ltd., Harmondsworth, Middlesex, 1970.(

3. Plato (Hamilton, Walter translated). 'The Phaedrus', 78, paragraph 264, in Plato (Hamilton, Walter translated), *Phaedrus and The Seventh and Eighth Letters*, 1-160, Penguin Books Ltd., Harmondsworth, Middlesex, 1973.

4. Freeman, Kenneth J (Redall MJ, Ed). *Schools of Hellas, An essay on the Practice and Theory of Ancient Greek Education from 600 to 300 BC*. Third Edition, MacMillan and Co. Ltd, London, 1922.

5. Orme, Nicholas. *Early British Swimming 55BC-AD1719, With the First Swimming Treatise in English, 1595*. 1595, 1-215, University of Exeter, 1983.

6. Orme, Nicholas. 'A Short introduction for to learne to Swimme', 113-215, Edward White, London, 1595, in ibid., *Early British Swimming 55BC- AD1719*, 1-215, University of Exeter, 1983.

7. Digby, Everard. *De Artenatandi libri duo quorum prior regulas ipsius artis, posterior vero praxin demonrationemque continent. Authore Everado Dygbeio Anglo in artibus Magistro*. 1587. EEBO Editions.

8. Ayriss, Chris. *Hung Out To Dry, Swimming and British Culture*. 1-160, www.lulu.com, 2012.

9. Parr, Susie, *The Story of Swimming*, 1-191, Dewi Lewis Media, Heaton Moor, Stockport, 2011. N.B. The lines from the poem quoted in the *The Story of Swimming*, 14, misses out the line " He could not away from me; nor would I from him."

10. Alexander, Michael (translated). *Beowulf*, 68, Penguin Books Ltd., Harmondsworth, Middlesex, 1973.

11. Parr, Susie. op. cit., 20-21.

12. Alexander, Michael. op. cit., Introduction, 9.

13. Thompson, Della (Ed). *The Oxford Compact English Dictionary*, 562, OUP, 1996; Macaulay, Thomas Babington. 'Lays of Ancient Rome, 1842', in *Lays of Ancient Rome & miscellaneous essays & poems*, 405-434, (including Introduction) Everyman's Library, Dent, 1910. (pages 432-433 quoted)

14. Peacham, Henry. 'The Compleat Gentleman', 216, Francis Constable. London, 1634. in *Peacham's Compleat Gentleman*, 216, Clarendon Press, Oxford, 1906.

15. Mulcaster, Richard. *Positions*, 95, Thomas Vautrollier, Ludgate, London, 1561. Reprinted in 1888 by Longmans, Green and Co., London, 1888 with an Appendix by Robert Hebert Quick.

16. Marlowe, Christopher. 'Hero and Leander', 1598, 205, (printed by Adam Islip for Edward Blunt 1598) in Gill, Roma (Ed). *The Complete Works of Christopher Marlowe*, Volume I, line 631-648 & 659-664, Clarendon Press, Oxford, 1987.

17. Mulcaster, Richard, op. cit., 96.

18. ibid.,

19. Locke, John. 'Some Thoughts Concerning Education', 1693 in Grant, Ruth W and Tarcov Nathan (Eds), *Some Thoughts Concerning Education and Of the Conduct of the Understanding*, 14, Hackett Publishing Co Inc., Indiana, Indianapolis, 1996.

20. Freeman, Kenneth J. (Rendall MJ, Ed), op. cit., 152.

21. Locke, John, op. cit., 14.

22. Jimack, PD, 'Introduction', xv, in Rousseau, Jean-Jacques, *Emile*,1762, Foxley, Barbara, translated, Everyman's Library, 1911, J M Dent & Sons Ltd., Reprinted Dutton, New York, USA, 1976.

23. Rousseau, Jean-Jacques, *Emile*, 1762, Foxley Barbara translated, ibid., 96-97.

24. Jimack, P D, Introduction, xv, ibid., xv; *see also*: Juvenal (Green Peter, translated). *The Sixteen Satires*, 104 AD, 217, Penguin, Harmondsworth, 1967. The Quote comes from the Tenth Satire

25. ibid.,

26. Guts Muths, Johann Christoph Friedrich, *Gymnastics for Youth: Or a Practical Guide To Healthful and Amusing Exercises or the Use of Schools. An Essay Toward the Necessary Improvement of Education, Chiefly as it Relates to the Body*, Preface, vii, Printed for J Johnson, St Paul's Churchyard, London, 1800.

27. ibid., Chapter X, 339-360.

28. McIntosh, Peter C. *Physical Education in England since 1800*, 82-83, Bell & Hyman, Revised and Enlarged Edition, London, 1968.

29. Guts Muths, Johann Christoph Friedrich, op. cit., 358.

30. Clias, P H Captain, *An Elementary Course of Gymnastic Exercises Intended to Develop and Improve the Physical Powers of Man with the Report Made to the Medical Faculty of Paris on the Subject and a New and Complete Treatise on the Art of Swimming*. Chapter IV, 145-180, Printed for Sherwood, Gilbert and Piper And J Hearne, Fourth Edition, London, 1825.

31. Dukes, Clement. *Health At School*. 219, Cassell & Company, Limited, New and Enlarged Edition, London, 1887; *see also*, Dukes, Clement. *Health At School*, 337, Third Edition, Revised, Enlarged and Illustrated, Rivington, Percival & Co., London, 1894.

32. ibid., 222-223. (1887)

34. Bingham, Alderman JH. *The Period Of The Sheffield School Board 1870-1903*, 42, JW Northend Limited, 1949.

35. ibid., 128-129.

36. Drury, JFW. *Drury's Manual Of Education with Special Reference to the Education Act, 1902*, 269, John Heywood, Manchester, 1903.

37. TNA Ed. 125/21, Minute 08/15104A, Extract from Minutes, Yorkshire, West Riding, Burley in Wharfedale, Main Street, Council School, No. 153.

38. ibid., *see* notes terminating 28 April 1909.

39. TNA Ed. 111/126, Letter from Newark Education Committee, 10 June 1904.

40. ibid.

41. ibid., Minute 04/19016, 12 and 13 July 1904. Robert Morant notes in his Minute dated 15 August 1904 that Minute 04/19016 was not technically correct. There are also references to an Edmonton, Minute 03/14688; Burton on Trent Minute 04/12299; Borough of Newark Minute 04/5456 BT.

42. ibid., Letter from the LGB, 18 July 1904.

43. TNA Ed. 111/213, Letter from County Borough of Hastings Education Committee, 22 November 1904, Minute Ed. 33707, 23 November 1904.

44. ibid.

45. TNA Ed. 125/21, Letter from Cornwall Education Committee 23 March 1905, Minute 5/5908A

46. Seaborne, Malcolm and Lowe, Roy. *The English School, its architecture and organisation*, Volume II 1870-1970, 36, Routledge & Kegan Paul, London, 1977.

47. Sachs, Frank. *The Complete Swimmer*, 259, Methuen & Co Ltd., London, 1912.

48. Hutt, CW. *Crowley's Hygiene of School Life*, 227, Sixth Edition, Methuen & Co Ltd., London, 1924.

49. Surrey History Centre, The *13th to 95th Reports of The Surrey Education Committee* (SEC), 13 February 1906 to 13 March 1923.

CHAPTER 1
SWIMMING AT THE DORKING BRITISH SCHOOL

"Mr Warner has kindly volunteered to teach swimming to such boys as have obtained their parents' permission to go to the Swimming Bath. The Time Table will, therefore, be slightly altered on Tuesdays and Thursdays. The first lesson will end at 2.35."[1]

Remarkably a few weeks before Mr Warner's offer to the Head Teacher of the Dorking British School, the following letter was published in the *Dorking Advertiser*:

"We would .....solicit your practical help in the promotion of ..... swimming and life-saving ..... The neglect of this subject....(by) parents and scholastic authorities who do not consider it to be their duty.....but.....with the aid of the press.....we should rapidly approach the ideal when swimming and life-saving would become so well recognised that it would soon form part of our national education......"[2] (*see* Appendix I for full text)

The letter was signed by a number of representatives of swimming clubs and William Henry, honorary secretary of the Life Saving Society, founded in 1891, who was joint author of "Swimming", one of a number of books in the Badminton series on *Sports and Pastimes*. Refer also to Appendix II concerning swimming and bathing in the London School Board including a letter to the London School Board on a scheme for swimming promoted by Henry and others. Originally the Life Saving Society was called the "Swimmer's Life-Saving Society".[3] It was incorporated as the Royal Life Saving Society in 1904.

The introduction of swimming in 1896 by Mr Warner at the Dorking British School, which operated under the auspices of the British and Foreign School Society, established in 1814, was part of a wider movement locally. Miss Ellen M Corderoy led the local campaign to modernise the school buildings, after it faced the prospect of closure by the Committee of the Privy Council on Education (Education Department), which sought to incorporate many of the religious schools into the State system. After the 1902 Act the school became the Powell-Corderoy School; Mr T E Powell being an outstanding financial contributor to the school's future.[4]

As well as the swimming class of 1896, other innovations like the May festivals were initiated, where the May Queen, and, later the school captain received a personal copy of the Bible from Miss Corderoy.[5]

Mr Warner's initiative was recorded in the *Dorking Advertiser*[6] where it announced that about forty boys were having swimming lessons at the Public Bath in Station Road, Dorking. The boys were admitted at a reduced price, smaller boys on Tuesdays and bigger ones on Thursdays.

A few days earlier Mr Warner reported to the managers that the swimming class was going on swimmingly. Thirty boys were attending on two evenings a week. They paid one penny each and the (Bath) Company charged 1¾d. so that ¾d. remained to be found.[7]

It was suggested at the meeting that the secretary found out if the Education Department provided a grant through the current code.[8] However, this seemed an unlikely possibility since Article 101b referred to a grant for Discipline and Organisation where physical exercises were timetabled. (*see* note 15 below). If this was not possible, Mr Cousin was asked to collect from well-wishers an amount between 20/- to 30/- in respect of payments that had to be made over and above the payments made by the boys.[9]

On 21 January 1897, Mr Warner's son, Charlie, died from a severe attack of laryngitis and bronchitis. The funeral was held on Tuesday, 26 January 1897. Subsequently, Miss Corderoy offered a silver medal in his memory respecting a one length competitive race for boys.[10] Four prizes were offered by several members of the committee to other successful competitors; Thomas Warner, Robert Woods, Ed. Woods and Harry Mills.

The silver medal was first won by Wesley Turner,[11] a boy in standard VII and the race and the award was thereafter competed for every year until 1938 (Appendix III) when the Urban District Council (UDC) Bath closed.

The progress of swimming at the school may be gauged from the fact that on Friday 1 September 1898, a gala was held at the Public Baths. Mr Warner was in charge of the races and Miss Corderoy gave the prizes.[12] Girls were not excluded from participating in the events:

The Programme	Prize Winners
1. Length race for girls	1. Kate Mills
	2. Rose Warner
2. Width race for girls	1. Annie Holman
3. Evening School 2 lengths lads race	1. G Walker
	2. W Turner
4. Exhibition of Diving, Swimming & Life-Savers by Messieurs E. Hubbard, Charl, B. Mills & C. Mills	
5. One length for boys for the "Charlie Warner" medal	1. Percy Jeal (C.W. Prize)
	2. Thomas Warner
	3. Fred Knight
6. Width race for boys	1. F Spencer
	2. J Cavan

During the season twenty certificates were awarded by the Baths Company to the boys and girls of the school. Nearly 700 tickets were issued to the scholars, parents, managers and scholars.

The next gala was held on 15 September 1899 and it was slightly more ambitious than the first.

Programme	Results
1. The "Charlie Warner" medal	1. Thomas Warner
	2. Norman Spratling
2. Width race	1. Harry Borer
	2. Sidney Spratling
3. Pole Walking	Percy Jeal
4. Girls Length race	1. Kate Mills (silver medal)
	2. Rose Warner
	3. Annie Holman
5. Girls Width race	1. Ethel Letts
	2. Ethel Shepherd

Swimming through the School Swimming Club appears to have begun in the second week of June in both 1899 and 1900. This seems rather late and it is not exactly clear why this was so, as several hypotheses might be postulated.

Nevertheless, the arrangements for the club in 1900 were:

Boys – Tuesdays and Thursdays at 4 o'clock

Girls - Wednesdays at 4 o'clock and Saturday at noon

Apart from the school's own gala, there was, on 12 September 1900, the Dorking Swimming Club Sports at which there was a School Team Race; the winners being the British School, followed by the High School and the National School. The Dorking British Team was composed of Percy Jeal, Norman Spratling and Horace Weeks. Each boy received a prize of a silver watch.[13]

The School's gala for 1900 apparently took place during the afternoon of Thursday, 13 September 1900 as the bath was lent by the proprietors for the purpose of holding the gala.[14]

Programme	Results
1. The "Charlie Warner" race (medal)	1. Norman Spratling
2. One length handicap boys	1. Thomas Warner
3. One length handicap girls	1. Denise Holman
4. One width boys	1. H. Jeal
	2. E. Lucock
5. One width girls	1. Elsie Warner
	2. Alice Butcher
6. Distance Race boys	1. W Jeal
	2. J Brazington
7. Distance Race Girls	------------
8. Comic Race (Bag Snatching)	1. H Weeks
	2. Kate Mills

9. Aquatic Tea Party by 4 boys and 2 girls
10. Diving by P Jeal, N Spratling, H Weeks, H Borer and T Warner
11. Life Saving

Prizes were distributed by Miss Corderoy.

Swimming training in 1901 began as usual in the second week of June. The times of the training are interesting in so far as the boys' timetable was from 11am to noon on Tuesdays and Thursdays while the girls swam from 4pm to 5pm on Wednesdays and noon to 1pm on Saturdays. The timetabling might, of course, have had something to do with available instructors, especially for the girls, or the availability of time at the baths. Whatever the reason, it is interesting to note that the boys' timetabling of swimming was during school time and it can only be assumed that this was allowed by the HMI, who may well have been J C Colvill.

The basis on which swimming may have been allowed in this instance was probably due to the code (*Code of Regulations for Day Schools with Schedules and Appendices*), of 1894, Article 12(f). This code noted what was termed "secular instruction" as the basis of instruction in certain subjects, such as *suitable physical exercises, e.g., Swimming, Gymnastics, Swedish Drill etc.; Military Drill (for boys) whether or not it was given on the school premises or by the ordinary teachers of the school, provided that special and appropriate provision approved by the Inspector was made for such instruction and the times for giving it were entered on the approved Time Table.* This 1894 code held until 1901 when suitable *physical exercises* was replaced and substituted in the 1901 code by the words *Physical Training.*[15] Nevertheless, Schedule III of the 1901 code noted that "*The Model Course of Physical Training for use in the Upper Departments of Public Elementary Schools*, (Model Course) which was then in the course of preparation, may be supplemented, where possible, by further and more varied Physical Training, including, where possible, systematic instruction in swimming , cricket etc." (But *see* Text with Note 45 in the Introduction) What this apparently boiled down to was the question of "attendance".[16] In 1907 the code restored swimming as an alternative to physical training.

However, the Education Department did not provide grants for swimming between 1894 and 1901 and, from 1902 until 1907 swimming could only be timetabled in any PES with the approval of the Board in certain circumstances (*see* Introduction). In 1902, for example, the Board refused to reconsider an application from the School Board for London, (The London Schools Swimming Association [LSSA]was formed in 1893 – *see* Appendix II), which was not abolished until 1903, to include practical instruction in swimming and life-saving in the water from the list of recognised subjects for grants[17] except for land drill. (The Board of Education was established by the Board of Education Act, 1899).

Nevertheless, in the Dorking British School, swimming was still reported[18] as commencing during school time for the boys between 11 and 12 Tuesdays and Thursdays while the girls trained at 4pm to 5pm on Wednesdays and noon to 1pm on Saturdays.

The printed programme for the 1901 Gala held on 25 September 1901, which started at 6.30pm may be found in the 1901 Log Book.[19] Admission prices were quoted as 6d. and 1/-. The gala was considerably expanded and included the following events:

1. Beginners Race (Boys)
2. Plunge* for the "Charlie Warner" Prize (a silver medal given annually by Miss Corderoy in memory of an old scholar, the son of Mr T C Warner) open to all scholars of the school. The boy obtaining the highest aggregate of marks for Plunging, Diving and Swimming secured the prize. The competitors were F Jeal, H Weeks, H Borer and Sidney Spratling.
   * Plunging was a standing dive made head first from a firm take off from spring. The body had to be kept motionless, face downwards, and no progressive actions

must be imparted to it other than the impetus of the dive. According to the laws of the Amateur Swimming Association the plunge was completed, if the competitor's face had not been already been raised above the surface of the water, at the expiration of sixty seconds, and the distance traversed in a plunge should be measured along a straight line, at right angles to the diving base, to a line parallel to the diving base, at the furthest point reached by any portion of the competitor's body.[20]

3. Comic Race. Lighted Candle and Costume
4. Width of Bath (Boys under 12), R Course, H Humby, N Cousin, W Rumbold, W Jeal.
5. Two lengths "Charlie Warner" Prize.
6. Life Saving T Warner, P Jeal, N Spratling

7. Width (Boys over 12) 2 Heats

1st Heat	2nd Heat
J Weller	B Stokes
H Shepherd	E Lucock
H Stokes	H Edwards
E Croucher	W Humby
A Skitt	

8. Comic Race, Cork Snatching
9. Final for width
10. Diving "Charlie Warner" Prize
11. One length handicap

1st Heat	2nd Heat	3rd Heat
F Jeal	H Weeks	T Warner
M Bacon	J Brassington	S Spratling
H Edwards	N Cousin	H Borer
H Shepherd	E Lucock	H Jeal
		W Jeal

12. Two lengths handicap for old "Britishers" who learned to swim while at school.
13. Beginners Race (girls)
14. Final one length handicap
15. Aquatic Tea Party

Percy Jeal	Host
F Jeal, H Borer, H Weeks, T Warner	Visitors
N Spratling, J Caven	Waiters

16. Diving - including Plunging, High Diving, Running Dive and picking up small coins from the bottom of the bath.

The winners of the races were written in, in the programme. It is clear that the UDC were issuing certificates for children in respect of certain successful distances swum but it is not known what those distances were.

The 1902 gala was held on Wednesday, 10 September 1902. As in Croydon's Elementary Schools, prizes were given to successful participants. Prizes had been given before 1902 but the 1902 gala seems to have begun a new phase in the expansion of prizes given. Although the races followed a familiar pattern the prizes were substantial:

1. Width for Beginners	1st Prize - Cricket Bat
	2nd - Cricketing Shirt
	3rd - Writing Case

1st & 2nd in each heat to swim in final

2. "Charlie Warner" medal-diving

3. One length handicap   1st Prize - Watch
                                            2nd - Silver Chain
                                            3rd - Stumps

4. Width-final

5. "Charlie Warner" medal - 2 lengths scratch

6. Two lengths handicap-for old boys

                                            1st Prize - Bag
                                            2nd - Military Brushes in Case
                                            3rd - Walking Stick
                                            2 heats

7. Comic Race   1st Prize - Cricket Bag
                                            2nd - Writing Case

8. One length for girls   1st Prize - Brooch
                                            2nd - Purse.

9. Width for girls   1st Prize - Hair brush
                                            2nd - Work Basket

10. "Charlie Warner" medal-Final 2 lengths

11. Running Dive   1st Prize - Book
                                            2nd - Football
                                            3rd - Writing Case

12. Old Boys Final

13. Two lengths handicap   1st Prize - Silver Chain
                                            2nd - Fishing Rod
                                            3rd - Book

14. Plunging   1st Prize - Compasses
                                            2nd - Clothes Brush

15. One length final

16. "Charlie Warner" medal-plunging

17. Two lengths handicap-final

18. Life Saving

19. Comic Race   1st Prize - Cricket Bat
                                           2nd - Ball

20. Diving by Old and Present Boys

The 1903 gala was held on Wednesday 16 September and commenced at 6.30pm. There was an innovative section of the programme insofar as a full list of officials was quoted. The prizes were given out by George Scales. The Starter was S Wild. Judges were TG Rix, TC Warner and H Shearburn. The referee was EW Attlee and the clerks of the course were Mr Cousins, the head teacher and Mr Wilson. There was again a full set of prizes for the eighteen events. There was an appreciation by the Committee for everyone who contributed to the success of the sports. The Committee asked for continued assistance, since the County Council made no grant for the teaching of this important subject. The reason why they did not do so may be explained by the confusion that emanated from the Board, the details of which may be found in the Introduction.

The 1904 gala (Appendix IV) took place on Wednesday 21 September at which there were fifteen races. The previous week at the UDC sports, the British school team had won the annual Challenge Cup presented by J Croft Deverell between Dorking's elementary schools. The British team boys are recorded as having won nineteen other prizes.[21]

The 1905 gala took place on Wednesday 20 September 1905 and had a total of twenty-one events:[22]

1. High Dive - 2 prizes
2. Width for Beginners - 2 prizes
3. Running Dive - 2 prizes
4. One length girls - 2 prizes
5. Plunging - 2 prizes
6. One length boys - 3 prizes
7. Two lengths scratch "Charlie Warner" medal
8. Comic race - 2 prizes
9. One length - final
10. Two lengths scratch - final
11. Two lengths handicap, old boys - 2 prizes
12. Singing under water
13. Three lengths boys, 2 prizes
14. Two lengths, old boys - 2 prizes
15. Extra Turn
16. Swimming under water
17. Three lengths final
18. Running Dive, old boys - 2 prizes
19. One length on the back - 2 prizes
20. Life Saving
21. Comic Race boys - tea party

A year later on Wednesday 19 September the 1906 gala had one event less than that of 1905:

1. Width race, girls - 2 prizes
2. One length handicap, girls - 2 prizes
3. One length handicap - 2 prizes
4. Width boys - one prize
5. Plunging - 2 prizes
6. Two lengths scratch - "Charlie Warner" medal
7. Diversions, Mr Large & the Master's Turner

8.   Three lengths handicap, old boys "A" - 2 prizes

9.   Four lengths handicap, old boys "B" - 3 prizes

10.   Running Dive - 2 prizes

11.   Two lengths handicap, girls who have left school

12.   Running Dive, old boys - 2 prizes

12A. High Dive (old boys) - 2 prizes

13.   Two lengths handicap - 3 prizes

14.   Four lengths final

15.   Swimming under water - 1 prize

16.   Two lengths final

17.   Swimming on the back - 2 prizes

18.   Plunging, old boys - 2 prizes

19.   Life Saving Display by Five old boys - winners of the medallion of the Royal Life Saving Society

20.   Comic Race, "A Walk In the Park" - 2 prizes

The 1908 swimming gala was the first to be held at the end of the summer term,[23] which also awarded a girls' championship medal for the first time (Appendix V). The gala reverted back to September in 1909. The Schools' competitions, however, apparently remained fixed in the early part of each new term throughout these early years as the British School won the Deverell Challenge Cup in October 1908. The 1909 and 1910 galas continued more or less in the same vein as previously, although in 1910 there were feet foremost races for boys and girls.

For the first time in 1910 the Log Books record the award of the SEC, local and Royal Life Saving Certificates of competence in swimming.[24]

The 1911 gala was reported as having been held on 1 August 1911 and a swimming examination for boys and girls to be held on the following Wednesday and Thursday by Dorking UDC.[25] The 1912 gala was held on the afternoon of 23 July 1912 while the 1913 gala reverted back to 5 September, and, on 29 September there was a half-holiday for swimming competitions. Swimming lessons in 1913 began on May 20: boys on Tuesdays from 11-12 noon and Thursdays 11:45 to 12:45: girls on Tuesdays 3-4pm and Fridays 11-12 noon. The swimming galas were continued throughout the First World War but in what form, from the SHC records, it is not possible to say, except that the "Charlie Warner" medal and the Girls' champion races were competitively continued.

The Log Books record that Mr Cousins, head teacher of the Boys' School was beginning his twenty-eighth year as Head Teacher in January 1920. On 26 July 1920 the swimming competition only involved the two championship medals, while the swimming gala proper was held on the afternoon of 5 October at 2:30pm.[26]

It should not be overlooked that village schools also played a prominent part in the promotion of swimming. According to Shalford School, 150 years of a Village School, 1855-2005, for instance, swimming began in 1902 with boys travelling to Guildford Baths, while in 1906 the school began to use the River Wey.[27] It seems clear that when the Superintendent observed, in the results of swimming for the particular year to which he was addressing in his yearly reports, that schools were swimming at no cost to the SEC, local facilities such as this were in use by the respective schools (*see* Chapter 4 for the swimming estimates for 1909). Nevertheless, the Dorking British School was just one of several schools in Dorking that began a tradition of swimming as part of its curriculum and extra-curricula activity. The swimming enterprise was naturally aided by the siting of a UDC bath in the town. Nevertheless, the schools did well to offer a progressive system of competition between them, which offered children of ability in swimming incentives to improve, and, perhaps, more important to them, prizes for their endeavours. Not only that, however, was the important attitude of the schools and the UDC to the possibilities of potential improvement to non-swimmers of either gender.

The significance of this to the wider child population in the Public Elementary Schools of Surrey was the appointment of Major Arthur Ormand Norman as Superintendent of Physical Training from the 20 June 1905. He was keen to develop swimming in Surrey's PES, and the subsequent relaxation of the education code in 1907, enabled swimming to be undertaken by the children of the PES as part of the PT curriculum. He was to base his endeavours for the introduction of swimming in the elementary schools on the traditions and processes that he had found in the Dorking schools.

Nevertheless, there were considerable difficulties. Suitable facilities for swimming throughout the County and the south-east generally were a frustrating problem. There were few open reaches of river in Surrey as a letter to *The Sportsman* from Mr Alex Divine, headmaster of Claymore School, Pangbourne, noted, which was reported in the *West Middlesex Times*:[28]

> "Over a stretch of about 100 miles, from Richmond to Oxford, there are only 40 bathing places of any kind. Of these, fourteen are private bathing places, and, therefore, the number available for the public is reduced to twenty-six, of which sixteen are provided by local authorities, two are owned by hotel-keepers, four are public places on the towing path."

Moreover, of the forty places overall, eleven were situated at Oxford and Windsor, leaving twenty-nine for the rest of the river, many of which were private and three of which were reported as badly kept or out of repair. Amongst other places there was no bathing place either at Chertsey or Staines but Egham had a shelter on the river bank above Wharton's boathouse. The letter went on:

> "It is to be hoped that that it will soon be publicly recognised that it is the duty of all who are charged with the education of the young to see that children are taught swimming and life-saving before leaving school....but the facilities are by no means many;..."[29]

In *The Complete Swimmer*, 1912, a list of Bathing Places throughout the country was published and a list of those for Surrey may be seen in Appendix VI.

A further problem was obtaining instruction for girls. The Dorking British School's Minute Book for 2 June 1901,[30] for instance, recorded that a teacher for the girls was mentioned and a member agreed to approach a lady to find out if she would be prepared to undertake it.

Furthermore, in the Superintendent's scheme for the introduction of swimming into the curriculum in 1907 there was a lack of interest from the Girls' schools, which was probably due to the lack of women teachers capable of teaching swimming. For these reasons, swimming in the elementary schools of Surrey, remained prior to 1907, independent, voluntary and spasmodic.

A good example of this apparently random approach to the art of swimming in the elementary schools of Surrey was the origins of swimming in Guildford's and Sutton's Elementary Schools, which may be found in Appendix VII.

Notes
1.   SHC, C/ES/115/2/1/1, 1 June 1896, Log Book, Dorking British School, 174.
2.   *The Dorking Advertiser*, 14 May 1896, 5.
3.   Sinclair, Archibald and Henry, William. *Swimming*, 214, Second Edition, Longmans, Green, and Co., London, 1894.
4.   Cousin, S, 'Miss E M Corderoy, An Appreciation'. Reprinted from the *Dorking and Leatherhead Advertiser*, 4 March 1938.
5.   ibid.
6.   op. cit., *The Dorking Advertiser*, 18 June 1896, 5.
7.   SHC, C/ES/115/1/1/2, 8 June 1896, Minute Book (NP)
8.   Education Department, *Code of Regulations for Day Schools* with schedules and Appendices, 1895, 20, Article 101(b).
9.   SHC, op. cit., C/ES/115/1/1/2.
10.   SHC, C/ES/115/1/6/10.
11.   SHC, C/ES/115/2/1/1, 1 November 1897, Log Book, 195.
12.   ibid., 204.
13.   ibid., 237.
14.   ibid.
15.   Education Department, *Code of Regulations for Day Schools* with Schedules and Appendices, 1894, Article 12(f), 3.
16.   Drury, JFW. *Drury's Manual of Education*, 269, John Heywood, Manchester, 1903.
17.   *Hansard*, Volume 107, 4th Series, 28 April to 12 May 1902, 5 May 1902, column 624.
18.   SHC, C/ES/115/2/1/1, 10 June 1901, Log Book, 247.
19.   ibid., 249-250.
20.   Hodder, Thomas Knowles (Ed.). *Daily Express Book of Popular Sports*, 439, Daily Express Publications, London, no date(nd) (1935?).
21.   SHC, op. cit., C/ES/115/2/1/1, 291.
22.   ibid., 299.
23.   ibid., 334.
24.   ibid., 353-354.
25.   ibid., 365.
26.   SHC, C/ES/115/2/1/2, C/ES/115/2/1/2, 5 October 1920, Log Book 2, 8-9.
27.   Dierden, Margaret and Barrett, Jane, *Shalford School, 150 years of a Village School 1855-2005*, 18, Shalford Infant School, Shalford, Surrey, GU4 8BY, 2005.
28.   *West Middlesex Times*, 7 September 1907, 6.
29.   ibid.
30.   SHC, C/ES/115/1/1/3, 24 June 1901, Minute Book.

CHAPTER 2
THE ORIGINS OF SWIMMING IN THE ELEMENTARY SCHOOLS OF SURREY

At item 4 of the Superintendent's 1st Report[1] to the Special Committee on Physical Training and Medical Inspection (Special Committee Cognate), Major Norman recommended that swimming should be recognised as part of the PT curriculum whenever possible. The Special Committee Cognate[2] recommended the adoption of the Superintendent's Report except those recommendations that related to anthropometrical measurements.

The Superintendent next raised the issue of swimming in his Report of 14 September 1906.[3] Where facilities existed, swimming should take the place of PT in the summer months. He noted that the Germans placed a very high value to the learning of swimming in the physical development of boys compared with other forms of PT. In Denmark all PT was suspended during the summer, and, the time saved, devoted to swimming where bathing facilities existed. The question was really one of expenditure and he requested permission to submit more detailed suggestions on a future occasion.

The recognition that swimming should be a recognised subject of instruction in the place of PT during the summer months, where facilities existed, was subsequently approved by the SEC[4] with a grant of £60 approved for the purpose. The SEC was acting upon the Report of the Elementary Education Sub-committee,[5] which, was, in turn, acting upon the Medical Inspection and Physical Training Sub-committee (MIPTS)* Report,[6] which recommended swimming for the upper standards in the timetables of the schools. The MIPTS actually recommended £50 to be allocated for the purpose with a further £10 allocation in respect of the training of teachers, who were in the present circumstances unable to give instruction in the subject. The sub-committee also referred to the fact that a small sum be required for the use of the Charterhouse Public School's Bathing Place by children of the Godalming schools.

It became clear to the Superintendent[7] that any scheme of organisation could only flourish on an inverse basis to the scheme he had inaugurated for Swedish Drill. Swimming could not involve all pupils for reasons of cost, organisational difficulties within schools, disrupted timetables and lack of facilities. This could only be done by teachers who were conversant with local circumstances.

For those reasons, Major Norman recommended that any money allocated was to be confined to the Upper Standards of Boys, i.e. Standards V, VI and VII, and, in certain circumstances, where it would be advisable to Standards VI and VII only and to the Upper Standard VII of Girls. The differing local conditions made it impossible to lay down hard and fast rules applicable to all.

* **Note**: MIPTS held its first meeting on 27 June 1906 as reported in Appendix E.2, pp. 1248-1252 in the 16th Report of the SEC, 31 July 1906 replacing the Special Committee Cognate.

Indeed, existing facilities for bathing were not very numerous and mainly confined to those towns which possessed a swimming bath. He did not consider open reaches of river as satisfactory places for bathing large numbers of children even though it might be customary. The question of supervision had to be considered and an open reach of river as a suitable place for curriculum recognition had to be treated with a certain degree of hesitancy. He recommended that following the precedent of many other education authorities where lessons were taken in school hours as part of the curriculum, the pupil be put to no expense, but the lessons should not exceed two baths a week.

Major Norman recognised the significance of the Dorking Schools in the development of swimming in those schools. Clearly, the Superintendent had consulted with those schools regarding the proposed organisation and cost. He noted that although no records were available, two baths a week for three months of the year had been the general rule for the Dorking Schools. Many children had been taught to swim, and were in possession of certificates for swimming and life-saving. The number of baths taken over the years had increased as:

School	1900	1905
Dorking, St Paul's School	164	1,295
Dorking, British School	722	1,075
Dorking, National School	438	857
Dorking, (Rural) Westcott School	116	377

One bath a week was taken in school hours, the other after school hours. At least one of the school staff attended both in and out of school hours and gave instruction in swimming. Nevertheless, in Dorking, as elsewhere in the County, there was difficulty in obtaining instruction for the girls. However, a great portion of the success of swimming for girls in Dorking was down to a lady called Miss Philps who devoted much of her time to helping school staff.

The cost of the baths had been defrayed on one occasion a week by the children or by the Managers of the schools. The town authorities in Dorking gave every encouragement to the children and admitted them at 1d a head, a considerable reduction from the ordinary rate. The UDC also gave prizes in the annual swimming competition it organised. The estimated cost of providing tickets for the Dorking Schools for 1907 were:

School	No	Baths a Week	Weeks	£ - s - d	
Dorking:					
British Boys	40	1	9	1-10-00	(360d)
British Girls	15	1	9	11-03	(135d)
National Boys	40	2	9	3-00-00	(720d)
National Girls	12	2	9	18-00	(216d)
St Paul's Boys	40	1	9	1-10-00	(360d)
St Paul's Girls	15	1	9	11-03	(135d)
(Rural) Westcott Boys	30	1	9	1-02-06	(270d)
(Rural) Westcott Girls	15	1	9	11-03	(135d)
				£9-14-03	

So, the Superintendent based his scheme on the existing schools where swimming was already included in the curriculum. Nevertheless, schools that did not include swimming in the curriculum were not ignored and he seems to have raised the subject of introducing swimming into schools with head teachers on his drill visits to schools. It is possible that he invited head teachers to exert pressure on managers. Mr Smith, headmaster of Egham Hythe Boys Council School (Appendix VIII), raised the question of swimming with the managers in a letter that was considered by them on 28 May 1907.[8] On 23 June 1907, Major Norman visited the school about the swimming class.[9] Subsequently, the head received notice that the boys could commence swimming lessons in the week of 15 July 1907. Ten swimmers and ten non-swimmers were to have lessons on Mondays and Fridays from 3.45pm to 5pm.[10]

It is indicative of the lack of facilities in the area that arrangements for the lessons were made at Messieurs Tim's Boatyard in Staines on the River Thames, which can be found today at the bottom of Timsway off Chertsey Lane. Similar arrangements were recommended for the Station Road Boys' School in Egham. The SEC agreed to an expenditure of £2. 13s. 4d. (640d),[11] which suggests, assuming that twenty boys from each school attended the lessons, with a cost of 1d. a lesson that they attended for eight weeks. These arrangements did not end until 1924, when an offer of Staines UDC was taken up to allow each school a group of twenty children to use the new children's swimming place and bathing platform at 1/- for each group.[12] As a result, the SEC sanctioned the payment of 10/- to the boatman who ferried the Station Road boys to the bathing station.[13]

In 1907, however, the cost was not always a consideration in the provision of facilities. In Godalming, voluntary bathing had been taking place on a reach by the river used by Charterhouse School, which was open at certain hours to the public. A diving board was situated there. The headmaster of Charterhouse was prepared to allow the elementary schools use of the reach for two periods a week. The Godalming National School accepted this offer and the staff of the school were able to give instruction (also Appendix VIII).

The Superintendent's general proposals were to provide for the use of swimming baths and facilities for one day a week for nine weeks. In the Farnham schools his proposals were based on swimming for over 700 boys and 165 girls for twelve weeks, since the Farnham schools apparently did not break up for holidays until September:

Farnham Schools	No. of Children	Baths a Week	No. of Weeks	£ - s - d	
East Street	40	1	12	2-00-00	(480d)
West Street	55	1	12	2-15-00	(660d)
Hale	40	1	12	2-00-00	(480d)
Badshot Lea	40	1	12	2-00-00	(480d)
Bourne	40	1	12	2-00-00	(480d)
St Polycarp	15	2	12	1-10-00	(360d)
National (girls)	Nil				
Windlesham	30	1	12	1-10-00	(360d)
Total No. of Baths = 3,300				**£13-15-00**	**(3,300d)**

At Frensham, the headmaster personally instructed boys twice a week in Frensham (Little) Pond and no expense was incurred. Pupils were examined in swimming and certificates of proficiency awarded.

The floating swimming bath at Walton-on-Thames was formerly used by the pupils of the Walton and Oatlands Schools but its use ceased apparently, when financial assistance, which had formally been granted, was withdrawn. Were the grant restored the teachers would have been prepared to adopt the following:

Walton-on-Thames Council School

Boys	40	1 bath	9 weeks
Girls	35	1 bath	9 weeks

Oatlands Council School

Boys	15	1 bath	9 weeks
Girls	3	1 bath	9 weeks

There is some confusion over the interpretation of the swimming facilities available to the girls of the Oatlands Council School in the Superintendent's Report[14] since he goes on to say, in respect of swimming for the boys of the Weybridge Council School and the girls of Oatland's Council School, that, they had, in the past used a reach of the Thames marked off and supervised by the local authority. The authority had offered, free of charge, to have their attendant, with a boat, always in attendance during the school bathing hours. The pupils, many of whom could swim already, were anxious to take advantage of this generous offer. The local authority assured the Superintendent that there would be little, if any risk, nevertheless, the Superintendent was unable to accept the responsibility of recommending its use for a class of elementary school children. What seems to have happened is that the floating bath came back into use with the Superintendent's inaugural scheme (*see* Chapter 3).

The Surbiton schools, although a long way from the Kingston Corporation Baths, made arrangements to take one swimming lesson a week in school hours. A party of boys from St Mark's School used the bath twice a week. (St Mark's was a non-provided school). School managers paid for their instruction and some 800 tickets were sold to the pupils the previous season. The swimming instruction was given by the headmaster and one member of staff. The Kingston Bath Authority was prepared to accept boys at 1d. per head per attendance but Kingston Baths had their own schools to cater for so the timetabled accommodation was limited:

Surbiton Schools	Nos	Baths a week	No. of weeks	£ - s - d	
Tolworth Council School	60	1	9	2-05-00	(540d)
Christ Church (Ch.Ch.) National School	30	1	9	1-02-06	(270d)
Long Ditton National School	30	1	9	1-02-06	(270d)
Ham National	20	1	9	0-15-00	(180d)
				£5-05-00	(1,260d)

Girls were not permitted during school hours but on an ordinary "ladies day", when the charge was sixpence the authority was prepared to accept threepence a head. Suggested arrangements were:

Long Ditton	20	1	9	2-05-00	(540d)
Tolworth	20	1	9	2-05-00	(540d)
				£4-10-00	**(1,080d)**

The Merton Schools

Suggested swimming for Merton was at the Wimbledon Baths although the difficulty of girls instruction was problematic.

Boys	40	2	9	3-00-00	(720d)
Girls	30	1	9	1-02-06	(270d)
				£4-02-06	**(990d)**

At Sutton only three hours a week were available each week, one for the boys and two for the girls. So, because of the time factor it was recommended that the three schools nearest to Sutton Baths – Crown Road, West Street and New Town – provided two parties of fifty pupils each. They were to utilise the time and the distribution of bath tickets each week at 1d. per head to a total number of 100 in proportion to the numbers for each school.

Sutton Boys

Crown Road}					
West Street }	100	1	9	£3-15-00	(900d)
New Town }					

The girls of the Sutton schools were unable to use the bath because of a lack of teachers with appropriate knowledge of swimming.

In the above scheme, the time devoted to swimming was to be taken during school hours. The attempt to carry it out was entirely dependent on the decision of the SEC in respect of the cost, which would inevitably become part of the school curriculum. In this respect, the Superintendent recommended the precedent set by the larger Leas, for example: London, (*see* Appendices II, IX and X for the development of swimming in the London School Board). Oldham, Chester, Manchester, Birmingham and other County Boroughs should also be followed.[15]

Notes

1. SHC, Appendix E.3, 21 December 1905, pp. 333-343 in *13th Report of the SEC*, 13 February 1906, pp.169-449.
2. SHC, Appendix E.1, 21 December 1905, pp. 319-320 in ibid., *13th Report.*
3. SHC, Appendix E.2, 14 September 1906, pp. 1734-1735 in *17th Report of the SEC*, 13 November 1906, pp. 1604-1854.
4. SHC, *19th Report of the SEC*, 14 May 1907, pp. 829-1094, 838.
5. SHC, Report of the Elementary Education Sub-committee, pp. 882-893, 887 in ibid., *19th Report.*
6. SHC, Appendix E.1, Report of the MIPTS, 10 April 1907, pp. 937-943, 937 in ibid., *19th Report.*
7. SHC, Appendix E.2, Report of the Superintendent of PT, 24 March 1907, pp. 946-958, 946-947 in ibid., *19th Report.*
8. SHC, C/EM/67/1, 28 May 1907, Minutes, 10.
9. Egham Hythe Boys School, Log Book, 13 June 1907, 284.

10.   ibid., 287.
11.   SHC, op. cit., C/EM/67/1.
12.   SHC, C/EM/67/4, 24 June 1924, Minutes, 24.
13.   ibid., 28 October 1924, 33.
14.   SHC, op. cit., Appendix E.2, 24th March 1907, in op.cit., *19th Report*.
15.   ibid.

CHAPTER 3
1907 – THE INAUGURAL YEAR OF SWIMMING
IN SURREY'S ELEMENTARY SCHOOLS

In spite of the fact that much of the swimming was undertaken in cold water and in the open air of a generally cold summer, 403 children learned to swim, of whom 342 were boys and sixty-one girls. Free tickets were a great help. Distribution to scholars in Standards VI and VII was not always the best use of the places available. Season tickets were occasionally a better way of allocating places, but this depended on local conditions. Teachers generally recommended that, in future, swimming should start on 1 May. Nine lessons were also considered insufficient, twelve being regarded as a more realistic number in the context of swimming development. There were also some requests for belts and wings to be available to school staff for help in their instruction of the children. A rope was asked for in one case in order to provide greater safety. None of these items were expensive, so, a request for funding was to be made in the next set of estimates.

Thirteen teachers attended classes of instruction in swimming. Six learned to swim, three of whom undertook the instruction of their pupils.

One of the problems encountered was that there was no standard of competence of what the term "able to swim" meant. This was because swimming took place in a range of facilities, such as indoor and floating baths, plus the small backwaters of ponds and rivers. Because of these anomalies, and, the fact that local baths tended to fix their own standard of measure, the Superintendent thought that thirty yards would be considered an appropriate distance for a certificate to be awarded.

The grants had contributed to the success of this inaugural year, but, were not the conclusive factor, since, there had been interest in the schools for many years. Moreover, the results obtained were largely the result of teachers training the scholars so that there was little expenditure on swimming instructors.[1] The Superintendent enclosed an appendix[2] (Appendix XI) to the main appendix detailing for each school brief remarks on the nature of the swimming undertaken by each school during the season, some of which are mentioned above.

Notes

1.   SHC, Appendix M.1., Report of the Superintendent of PT., 2 January 1908, pp. 418-427 in *22nd Report of the SEC*, 11 February 1908, pp. 183-446.
2.   ibid.

CHAPTER 4
SWIMMING IN 1908 TO 1910

In his swimming estimate for 1908,[1] the Superintendent noted that the increase of £15 to £75 over the 1907 estimate was chiefly due to the extension of swimming lessons from nine to twelve for the season, for the inclusion of other schools and the provision of necessary apparatus.

There was no allocation of money in respect of payment for instruction except that by Messrs Tims of Staines and Clark of Walton-on-Thames.

The estimates were again based on a 1d. charge, the detail of which was:

Dorking District		Nos	Weeks	Total Tickets	£ - s - d
Dorking, Powell-Corderoy, (formerly British)					
	Boys	40	12	480	2-00-00
	Girls	15	12	180	0-15-00
Dorking, C of E					
	Boys	40	12	480	2-00-00
	Girls	15	12	180	0-15-00
Dorking, St Paul's C of E					
	Boys	40	12	480	2-00-00
	Girls	15	12	180	0-15-00
Dorking (Rural) Westcott C of E					
	Boys	30	12	360	1-10-00
	Girls	15	12	180	0-15-00
Farnham District					
Farnham					
East Street Council		40	12	480	2-00-00
West Street Council		50	12	600	2-10-00
St Polycarp's (RC) Roman Catholic.		30	12	360	1-10-00
(Rural), Hale Council		40	12	480	2-00-00
(Rural), Badshot Lea Council		40	12	480	2-00-00
(Rural), Bourne Council		40	12	480	2-00-00
(Rural), Wrecclesham, C of E		30	12	360	1-10-00

Surbiton District

Surbiton					
Hill Road, Ch. Ch., P		30	12	360	1-10-00
Hook, St Paul's		20	12	290	1-00-00
St Andrew's Road					
C of E		30	12	360	1-10-00
Tolworth, Council		60	12	720	3-00-00
St Matthew's		20	12	240	3-00-00
Long Ditton, C of E		30	12	360	1-10-00
New Malden		20	12	240	1-00-00
Ham					
	Boys	30	12	360	1-10-00
	Girls	15	12	180	2-05-00

Sutton District

Sutton					
Benhilton C of E		30	12	360	1-10-00
Crown Rd.*,Council					
	Boys,	40	12	480	2-00-00
	Girls,	30	12	360	1-10-00
New Town, Council					
	Boys	40	12	480	2-00-00
	Girls	30	12	360	1-10-00
West Street, Council		25	12	300	1-05-00
**Merton **		40	12	480	2-00-00

Horley

Lumley Road Council	-	-	60	1-10-00

Egham District

Egham			
Hythe, Council,	20}	Twice each week	
Station Road,Council 20 }		during season	4-04-00

Walton-On-Thames District

Walton-on Thames, Council	}	9	
Boys 7/6 per week}			
Girls	}		
Oatlands, Council	}	9	
Boys	}		
Girls 7/6 per week }			6-15-00
Mortlake, Council	40	12	480	2-00-00

	Total			**66-09-00**
	Training of Teachers			4-00-00
	Provision of Apparatus			2-00-00
	Incidental Expenses			2-11-00
	Total			**75-00-00**

*Quoted as Cromer Road

** No further designation given

The allocation of tickets was to be allocated on a seasonal basis where circumstances demanded it, bearing in mind the fact that the SEC required as many children as possible to learn to swim. Swimming lessons, therefore, did not have the purpose of preparing children for the winning of challenge cups as their rationale.

The Superintendent noted that a swimming certificate ought to be available based on a kind of continuous assessment:

CERTIFICATE OF PROFICIENCY IN SWIMMING

This is to certify that...
has been examined and successfully passed the County swimming test.

Distance swum...................yards   Date.............................

....Head Teacher

	Distance	Head Teacher's Initials
19........	50 yards	....
19........	80 yards	....
19........	150 yards	....

Secretary

In the same report, the Superintendent recommended some tips entitled:

FOR THOSE WHO WISH TO SWIM

1. Don't wait to get *cool* before entering the water.
2. Wet the *whole* of the body as soon as possible.
3. Keep the head thrown back.
4. Rest the *chin* on the *top* of the water.
5. Try to swim as *low* as possible.
6. Keep the stroke an *inch* under water.
7. Hollow the trunk nicely.
8. Don't hump up your back.
9. *Never* let the hands pass behind the bend of the elbow.
10. Shoot out the hands when the feet come together.
11. Breathe OUT when hands are in front.
12. Breathe IN when hands press backwards.
13. Make all your strokes *Slowly* and *Easily*.[2]

Those instructions would suggest that the swimming stroke taught to the children was the Breast Stroke.

In a further report,[3] chaired by JC Colvill, it was suggested, in one of the seventeen items proposed, that two hours a week was appropriate in a well-arranged curriculum for PT and that swimming and organised games should be considered as PT for this purpose. The minimum time that should be devoted to PT was 100 minutes or twenty minutes per day and regulations were issued accordingly.

Owing to the death of Major Norman due to overwork on 19 August 1908, Sergeant Mills, Assistant Instructor of PT reported[4] that 1,232 children – 978 boys and 254 girls – were instructed during the season, of which 522 – 430 boys and 92 girls – learned to swim.

Following Major Norman's death, Captain JE Mignon, Leicestershire Regiment, took up his duties on 17 December 1908.[5]

In 1909, when the swimming estimate increased by £55 to £130, Captain Mignon attempted to control the issue of free tickets. He suggested that head teachers should keep counterfoil books noting on each ticket the date of the class, the number of pupils attending the bath and the teacher in charge. They would sign the duplicate in the counterfoil providing a simple check on the number of tickets used by their school. As to baths which issued tickets, he suggested that a number approximate to that required, be issued by the official to the head teacher, and any left at the end of the season be returned and credited.[6] Nevertheless, the number of schools, as the increase in the monetary estimates suggest, expanded to a total forty-six schools plus a further seven, which represented no cost to the SEC. The cost was still based on a charge of 1d, and, in the case of most schools, a twelve-week course.

	Boys	Girls	Tickets		£ - s - d
Dorking District					
Powell Corderoy	40		960		£4-00-00
		30	360		1-10-00
Dorking C of E	40		960		4-00-00
		30	360		1-10-00
St Paul's C of E	40		480		2-00-00
		40	480		2-00-00
Westcott C of E	36		432		1-16-00
		30	360		1-10-00
Coldharbour RC	<10>		120		0-10-00
Farnham District					
East Street Council	40		480		2-00-00
		20	240		1-00-00
West Street Council	40		480		2-00-00
St Polycarp's RC	22		440	(10 weeks)	1-16-08
		6	120	(10 weeks)	0-10-00
Farnham Rural					
Hale Council	20		240		1-00-00
Badshot Lea Council	40		400	(10 weeks)	1-13-04
Bourne Council	24		240	(10 weeks)	1-00-00
		12	120	(10 weeks)	0-10-00
Wrecclesham C of E	20		240		1-00-00

Surbiton District

Surbiton Hill, Ch. Ch.	25		600	2-10-00
St Paul's, Hook	18		216	0-18-00
		8	96	1- 4-00
St Andrew's Road, C of E	40		600	2-10-00
		20	400	1-13- 4
Tolworth Council	30		720	3-00-00
Tolworth, St Mathew's	30		300	3-15-00
New Malden Council	12		144	0-12-00
		20	240	1-00-00
New Malden C of E	15		250	2-10-00
Ham	36		360	1-10-00
		14	140	0-11- 8
Long Ditton, C of E	40		480	2-00-00

Sutton District

Benhilton, C of E	30		360	1-10-00
		10	120	0-10-00
Crown Road Council	30		360	1-10-00
		30	360	1-10-00
New Town, Council	25		300	1-05-00
		25	300	1-05-00
West Street, Council	25		300	1-05-00

Merton & Mitcham

Merton C of E	75		900	3-15-00
		24	288	1-04-00
Singlegate, Council	35		420	1-15-00
Lower Mitcham Council	50		1,000	4-03-04

Wallington District

Wallington, Holy Trinity C of E	40		480	4-00-00
		40	480	4-00-00
Bedlington and Wallington C of E	10		120	1-00-00
		8	96	0-16-00

Horley District

Lumley Road, Council	60		60	1-10-00

Egham District

Egham Hythe Council	40		(once a week) }	
		20	(twice a week)}	
			} 8-08-00	
Egham Station Road Council	40		(once a week) }	
		24	(once a week) }	

Walton District

34

Walton-on-Thames Council	25			(Boys and)}	
				(Girls 7/6)}	
		20		(per week)}	
				}	
Walton-on-Thames, Oatlands Council	6			Ditto }	9-00-00
				Ditto }	
		6		Ditto }	
		}			
Walton-on-Thames, Hersham Council	20			Ditto }	

Barnes and Mortlake District

Barnes, Westfield Council	40		80	4-00-00
		20	240	2-00-00
Barnes Green, Council	20		240	2-00-00
Mortlake Council	40		480	4-00-00
		20	240	2-00-00
Mortlake, RC,	20		240	2-00-00
		20	240	2-00-00

Guildford District

Merrow C of E	20		240	1-00-00
				120-17-02
		Training of Teachers		6-00-00
		Apparatus		2-00-00
		Contingencies		1-02-10
				130-00-00

Additionally, Swimming would also take place at the following schools but without any cost to the SEC:

Epsom C of E
Epsom Council
Ewell C of E
Godalming C of E — Boys 40
Shalford Council — Boys 50
Shere
Holmbury St Mary's — Boys 18
— Girls 16
Sutton Belmont — Boys 30

The breakdown of cost for each district was:

Dorking	£18-16-00
Farnham	£12-10-00
Surbiton	£22-04-10
Sutton	£8-15-00
Merton	£10-17-04
Wallington	£9-16-00
Horley	£1-10-00

Egham	£8-08-00
Walton	£9-00-00
Barnes	£18-00-00
Guildford	£1-00-00
	£120-17-02

Along with the application of the estimate of expenditure for the summer of 1909, Captain Mignon noted in his report that he was enclosing a copy of a circular letter which he had sent to the Managers of those schools which took swimming last year. A similar letter with the necessary alterations was also sent to other schools which appeared to possess the essential facilities for swimming.[7]

Schedule C

> South Bank,
> Farnham Road,
> Guildford,
> 1st. March, 1909

....School

Swimming

Dear Sir,

In order to obtain the necessary information for the completion of the arrangements for Swimming during the coming season, and for the preparation of estimates for 1909-1910, I should feel much obliged if you would kindly inform me whether it is proposed to take this subject at the above School (a) again this year, and if so, would ask the Head Teacher or Teachers to fill in the information asked for in the accompanying Schedule.

In connection with this matter, I would draw your Managers' attention to the following points:-

1. Classes for Swimming should not be larger than the Teacher can thoroughly control and instruct, except where a number of scholars can swim, these being able to assist as Monitors.
2. All Classes should be accompanied by a Teacher who can swim and instruct the children, unless other suitable arrangements can be made.
3. The object of the Committee is not to specialise, but that as many new scholars as possible should be taught to swim.
4. The practice of issuing season tickets to be paid for by the Committee should therefore be discontinued.
5. Far better results may be looked for from two lessons a week than from one.

Full particulars of the arrangements made in previous years are not available, and as the estimates for the year 1909-1910 come before the Committee in the beginning of April, I should be much obliged if you would let me have a reply as soon as possible with the information asked for.

> Yours faithfully,
> JG Mignon, Captain.
> Superintendent of Physical Training.

To the Clerk or Correspondent.

Schedule Re Swimming

....School

....Department.

1. Number of Scholars who will attend   1...............................
   Swimming during 1909 session

2. Total number of tickets required   2...............................
   (If a Mixed Department, please give
   above information for Boys and Girls separately).

3. The name of the Baths used by the   3...............................
   School, or if no Baths, what arrangements
   have previously been made.

4. Name of responsible official to whom   4...............................
   communications may be addressed.

5. Distance of Bath or Swimming Place   5...............................
   from School.

6. Cost of tickets, or charge for use of   6...............................
   Swimming Place

7. Whether two lessons per week can be   7...............................
   taken.

8. If no member of staff can swim, names   8...............................
   of Teachers willing to learn, and facilities
   for their doing so.

9. What apparatus belonging to School or   9...............................
   available at Baths

10. If any additional apparatus is required   10...........................
    please specify.

11. Any other information:--   11...........................

Date....................................1909

.................................Head Teacher

At the end of the 1909 season, forty-two schools had taken part in the swimming scheme. Of these, nine schools were newcomers to the scheme. There were six girls' departments new to the scheme where previously only boys' departments of the schools concerned had participated. Three of the schools for which provision had been made in the estimates were unable to attend. The net increase in schools swimming over last year was eight and of departments twenty-one. The total number of pupils attending was 1,919 of whom 1,351 were boys and 568 girls.

The season produced 552 boys and 194 girls who learned to swim. Of these 385 gained certificates, 310 boys and seventy-five girls. The total cost was within the predicted estimates.

Much of the swimming was in the open air which was affected by bad weather throughout the season. Moreover, various epidemics closed down schools throughout the season.

Two boys, who had learned to swim, saved lives. The grant was undoubtedly helpful in the development of swimming, but, some schools that received no grant were equally keen on swimming. The success of the season's swimming was due in large part to the zeal displayed by head teachers and their staffs, and, in some cases valuable help was received from external sources.

Nine teachers received swimming instruction, of whom five learned to swim.

The 385 certificates were in the process of preparation and the continuous endorsement philosophy was a distinct incentive to do even better next year.

The final analysis of the 1909 season's results were:---(Appendix XII)

In January 1910[8] the Superintendent detailed the previously estimated expenditure for 1909 with the actual expenditure:

District		Estimate	Actual
Dorking		£18-16-00	£20-15-08
Farnham		12-10-00	12-10-00
Surbiton		22-04-10	17-10-00
Sutton	£8-15-00}	18-11-00	13-18-04
Wallington	9-16-00}		
Merton-Mitcham		10-17-04	5-12-08
Horley		1-10-00	1-10-00
Egham		8-08-00	6-06-00
Walton		9-00-00	10-10-00
Barnes-Mortlake		18-00-00	16-00-08
Merrow		1-00-00	Nil
Totals		**£120-17- 02**	**£104-13-04**

Training of Teachers-Swimming

	Estimate	Actual
Barnes, Westfield, Girls		1-10-00
Wallington, Holy Trinity, Girls		0-15-00
Sutton, Crown Road		0-10-00
Sutton, West Street		0-08-00
Farnham		0-15-00
Surbiton, St Andrew's Road		0-10-06
Hook, St Paul's		0-10-06
	£6-00-00	**£4-19-00**

Apparatus

	Estimate	Actual
Farnham	£2-00-00	12-04

Contingencies

Estimate	Actual
£1-02-10	Nil

During 1910 the MIPTS was reconstituted as the Medical Inspection (MI) Sub-committee. The work of PT in the elementary schools was transferred to the Elementary Committee and dealt with by a sub-committee of the Elementary Committee, the School Management sub-committee.[9] As far as instruction in Teachers' classes was concerned, this aspect was transferred to the Higher Committee along with work in Evening Continuation Schools and Secondary Schools.

Subsequently, the MI Sub-committee recommended that cases of life saving by children attending County swimming classes be reported to the Royal Humane Society and that certificates be awarded to the children so reported.[10]

The estimate for swimming increased to £150 (Appendix XIII) for the summer of 1910. This amount was £20 more than the previous year's estimate but £20 had been saved from the previous year's estimate.[11]

The Superintendent added a further five schools to the estimates owing to the opening of the new open-air baths at Woking, although the breakdown of the swimming results appeared to show the participation of six Woking schools, one of which, Westfield Council, had nine boy participants, which may explain the discrepancy of nine swimmers in the overall total number of participants.[12]

Subsequently, the Superintendent reported that fifty-seven schools, eighty-five Departments, fifty-five boys and thirty girls had taken part in swimming as part of the curriculum during the summer of 1910 (Appendix XIV). Two schools and one Girls' Department, for which provision had been made in the estimates were unable to attend.[13] The number of children under instruction was 1,688 boys and 609 girls. The total number of children who learnt to swim was 1,098, 809 boys and 289 girls. The number of certificates awarded was 518, 411 boys and 107 girls. Five teachers received swimming instruction.

Captain Mignon decided that the test of 'being able to swim' was contentious and that the standard of measure previously established was difficult to maintain and may even have fallen into disrepute. He, therefore, established the measure of ten yards as the distance required to qualify a pupil as having learnt to swim and a distance of thirty yards as the qualifying measure for the award of a certificate, which came into effect during the 1911 season.[14]

As well as the publication of results, Captain Mignon also set out the actual expenditure as opposed to the estimated expenditure (Appendix XIII details estimated expenditure for each school) for each of the districts in the summer of 1910:[15]

Districts	Estimated	Expenditure
Dorking	£21-10-00	£24-15-00
Farnham	£13-16-00	£11-16-00
Surbiton	£25-15-00	£25-10-00
Sutton-Wallington	£14-15-00	£14-05-00
Merton-Mitcham	£11-03-04	£11-04-01
Reigate	£02-06-08	£02-06-08
Horley	£01-10-00	£01-10-00
Egham	£06-06-06	£06-06-00
Walton	£10-10-00	£04-04-00
Barnes-Mortlake	£18-00-00	£20-13-04
Woking	- - - - -	£01-06-07
Totals	**125-12-00**	**123-16-08**

Training of Teachers

Barnes Westfield Girls		1-10-00
Weybridge C of E Girls		1-01-00
Mitcham Singlegate Girls		0-10-06
Merton C of E Girls		0-10-06
Dorking C of E Girls		2-00-00
Surbiton Hill Christ Church Boys		0-10-06
	10-00-00	**6-02-06**

Apparatus

Weybridge C of E Boys	0-05-06	
Woking Goldsworth Road Boys	0-19-04	
	5-00-00	1-04-10

Contingencies

Merstham	0-14-08	
Dorking	1-00-00	
Sutton	1-00-00	
Frensham	0-10-00	
Lower Mitcham	0-10-00	
	9-08-00	3-14-08

Summary

Use of Baths	125-12-00	123-16-08
Training of Teachers	10-00-00	6-02-06
Apparatus	5-00-00	1-04-10
Contingencies	9-08-00	3-14-08
	150-00-00	134-18-08

So overall a saving of £15-01-04 was effected.

Notes

1. SHC, Appendix M.3, Report of the Superintendent of PT, nd, pp. 150-174, Schedule A and Schedule B, in *23rd Report of the SEC*, 12 May 1908.
2. ibid.
3. SHC, Appendix E.1, Report of the Special Sub-Committee appointed to consider the Curriculum of Elementary Schools, 26 February 1908, pp. 326-334, in *24th Report of the SEC*, 28 July 1908, 332.
4. SHC, Appendix M1, Report of the Assistant Instructor of PT, 30 September 1908, pp. 618-619 in *25th Report of the SEC*, 10 November 1908.
5. SHC, Appendix M.1., Reportof the Superintendent of PT, 31 January 1909, pp. 973-975 in *27th Report of the SEC*, 16 March 1909, 975.
6. SHC, Appendix M1, Report of the Superintendent of PT, Schedule B, 26 March 1909, pp. 101-112 in *28th Report of the SEC*, 11 May 1909, 103.
7. SHC, Appendix M1, Report of the Superintendent of PT, Schedule C, 26 March 1909, 111-112 in ibid., *28th Report*.
8. SHC, Appendix M2, Report of the Superintendent of PT, 27 January 1910, pp. 1062-1063 in *32nd Report of the SEC*, 15 March 1910.
9. SHC, *33rd Report of the SEC*, 10 May 1910, 6.
10. SHC, Report of the MI Sub-committee, 31 March 1910, 66 in ibid., *33rd Report*, 10 May 1910.
11. SHC, Appendix MI, 22 March 1910, pp. 117-121 in ibid., *33rd Report*, 10 May 1910.

40

12. SHC, Schedule B, Report of the Superintendent of PT, in Appendix E.4, Report of the School Management Sub-Committee 3 May 1910, 24 May 1910 and 14 June 1910, pp. 372 in *34th Report of the SEC*, 26 July 1910, pp.215-460.
13. SHC, Schedule B, Report of the Superintendent of PT, 23 November 1910, pp. 773-785 in Appendix E.3 Report of the School Management Committee, 30 November 1910, pp. 745-786 in *36th Report of the SEC*, 10 January 1911, 774.
14. ibid.
15. SHC, Appendix E.3, Schedule C, 2 February 1911, pp. 878-879 in *37th Report of the SEC*, 14 March 1911.

CHAPTER 5
SWIMMING IN 1911

Captain Mignon estimated £165 as the expenditure for the 1911 swimming season. The increment was necessary because of the addition of new schools plus the Girls' departments of the Woking schools. Notably he considered it advisable to assess the estimates on a district by district basis for the season rather than school by school:[1]

District	Estimate
Dorking	£25-00-00
Farnham	£15-00-00
Surbiton	£30-00-00
Sutton	£15-00-00
Merton-Mitcham	£15-00-00
Reigate	£03-00-00
Horley	£01-10-00
Egham	£06-06-00
Walton	£04-04-00
Barnes-Mortlake	£20-00-00
Woking	£05-00-00
	£140-00-00
Instruction	10-00-00
Apparatus	5-00-00
Contingencies	10-00-00
Total	**£165-00-00**

On Wednesday 24 May 1911, the Superintendent attended a swimming gala at the Sutton Baths which he described as an admirable display.[2] The gala took place because of the successful endeavours of Mr Holland, a member of the SEC, to obtain a challenge shield for competition by the Sutton schools and to the donors, Mr Russell Davis and Messrs W Pile Ltd. (Proprietors of the Sutton Herald) (*see* Appendix VII).

Captain Mignon reported that sixty-five schools had taken part in the swimming season for 1911.[3] This involved sixty-two boys' departments and thirty-seven girls', ninety-nine in all. Three of the girls' departments were unable to attend during the season. The nett increase of schools' swimming during the 1911 season over that of 1910 was eight and of departments fourteen. The nett increase of children attending over the previous year was thirteen, of those who learned to swim twenty-seven, and, of those gaining certificates, ninety-nine. This year, the average number of pupils was 2,310 of whom 1,722 were boys and 588 girls. The total number who learned to swim was 1,125, 931 boys and 194 girls. Of these, 617 gained County certificates, 539 boys and seventy-eight girls. In addition 250 certificates were endorsed, 200 boys and fifty girls (Appendix XV).

The Superintendent reminded the SEC that fifty yards was the measure of achievements for a certificate to be awarded against that of thirty yards formerly and ten yards the adopted measure for 'learned or taught to swim' as against previously – a few strokes only.

The average attendance was only slightly in excess of the previous year but was in reality much greater because a strict average was now applied whereas before all the children attending was shown.

The Superintendent also pointed out the increase in the number of schools swimming from 1908 to 1911:

	1908	1911
No. of Schools	34	65
No. of Departments	45 (33 boys, 12 girls)	99 (62 boys, 37 girls)
No. of children	1,232 (978 boys)	2,310 (1,722 boys)
	(254 girls)	(588 girls)

Additionally, Captain Mignon reported that Frederic Collins of the Egham Hythe School and Leonard Kellow of Merton C of E were awarded the the Royal Humane Society's certificate for Life Saving, both having saved the lives of school fellows. Percy Apps of the Lumley Road School, Horley also saved the life of a school fellow but unfortunately it was during the school holidays when there were apparently no witnesses, at least not in the first instance.

Subsequently, the Superintendent announced a saving of £13-08-02 under the estimated total of £165 for the season's swimming.[4]

Notes

1. SHC, Appendix E.3, Report of the School Management Sub-committee, 24 March 1911, pp. 85-105, Schedule D, in *38th Report of the SEC*, 9 May 1911, pp. 1-131.
2. SHC, Appendix E.2, Schedule B, Report of the Superintendent of PT, 4 June 1911, p.261 in *39th Report of the SEC*, 25 July 1911, pp. 145-362.
3. SHC, Appendix E.2, Schedule B, Report of the Superintendent of PT, 24 November 1911, pp. 676-677 in *41st Report of the SEC*, 9 January 1912.
4. SHC, Appendix E.2, Report of the School Management Committee, 6 February 1912, pp. 796-814 in *42nd Report of the SEC*, 12 March 1912.

CHAPTER 6
SWIMMING IN 1913

One hundred and twenty eight departments – seventy-six boys and fifty-two girls – from eighty schools took part in swimming during the 1913 season. Three schools (five Departments), for which provision in the estimates was made, were unable to attend. This was an increase of twenty departments over the previous year.

There was a nett increase of children of 404. The total number of children who attended the swimming lessons was 2,893 of whom 1,895 were boys and 998 girls. The total number learning to swim, exclusive of those who gained county certificates was 764, 491 boys and 273 girls. The total number gaining county certificates was 667, 504 boys and 163 girls. Additionally, 302 children, 239 boys and sixty-three girls had their certificates endorsed.[1] The results of swimming in 1913 may be seen in Appendix XVI.

Notes

1. Appendix E.2, Report of the Superintendent of PT on Swimming, 28 November 1913, pp. 780-793, in *51st Report of the SEC*, 13 January 1914.

CHAPTER 7
SWIMMING TO 1922

The First World War inevitably took its toll of swimming. Many of the male teachers had gone off to war with inevitable consequences for physical curricula and extra-curricula activity. In 1917, twenty-nine schools, embracing forty-seven departments, took swimming as a subject for the curriculum. Several other schools used the baths out of school hours. The number of pupils who attended was 1,166, 716 boys and 450 girls. Six hundred and thirty-six children learned to swim, of whom 301 gained County certificates and 107 had their certificates endorsed.[1]

It should be noted that as a result of Colonel Mignon's death in the First World War, Miss Dorothy Le Couteur, the Assistant Superintendent, was appointed as Organiser of PT on the County Inspection Staff as from 1 January 1917. Her salary was increased to £200. Miss Le Couteur was under the general supervision of the County Inspector.[2]

Through 1918, forty-four schools representing sixty-eight departments took swimming as part of the school curriculum. No record was kept of extra-curricula swimming during the year. The number of pupils who attended was 1,670; 998 boys and 672 girls. Five hundred and fifty-five children learned to swim, 348 boys and 207 girls. Three hundred and forty-one received County certificates and 154 had their certificates endorsed.[3]

By Section 26(1) of the Education Act, 1918, no fees or other charges of any kind could be charged in any PES except as provided by the Education (Provision of Meals) Act, 1906 and the Local Education Authorities (Medical Treatment) Act, 1909.[4] A revision of the arrangements for instruction in swimming was, therefore, made necessary. For the 1920 season of swimming the SEC undertook to pay the travel expenses from the school to the bathing place where the distance of the exceeded two miles or less in exceptional circumstances. The SEC directed that sufficient time was to be allowed for the return journey to be made on foot.[5]

By 1922, swimming had recovered somewhat with ninety-three schools, 160 departments, ninety boys and seventy girls, participating in swimming during the season. Ten schools were new to taking part. The number of children who attended instruction was 3,730, of whom 998 learned to swim with 736 awarded certificates. A table of the development of swimming from 1907-1922 may be seen at Appendix XVII. The Leon trophy, presented by Mr AL Leon, for the south-western district was won by Godalming C of E School and the Richmond Cup by the Mortlake Boys' Council School.[6]

Notes

1. SHC, Report of the Organiser of PT, pp.136, in Elementary Education, pp. 134-139, in *71st Report of the SEC*, 12 March 1918, pp. 121-139.
2. SHC, *66th Report of the SEC*, 31 July 1917, 469-528, 495.
3. SHC, Elementary Education, pp. 150-155, 152 in *75th Report of the SEC*, 11 March 1919.
4. Barlow, Sir Montague, KBE, LLD, MP, & Holland, Richard. *The Education Act, 1918*, pp. 74, National Society Depository, London.
5. SHC, *82nd Report of the SEC*, 27th July 1920, pp.747-816, 769.
6. SHC, *95th Report of the SEC*, 13th March 1923, pp.261-319, 282.

CHAPTER 8
CONCLUSION

The Board, particularly after the final of the three Reports of the Royal Commission to enquire into the working of the Elementary Education Acts 1886-1888, (Cross Commission)[1] responded positively to the notion of change required in the concept of physical education/training to the purely militaristic concept which had gone before. The fact was that secular instruction was associated with the notion of attendance:[2]

"Article 12. "An attendance" means attendance at secular instruction.
Article 12 (f) In making up the minimum time constituting an attendance there
may be reckoned time occupied by instruction in any of the following
subjects, whether or not it is given in the school premises, or by the ordinary
teachers of the school, provided that special and appropriate provision
approved by the Inspector is made for such instruction, and the times for
giving it are entered in the approved Time Table:-

......
......
......

Suitable physical exercises, e.g., Swimming, Gymnastics, Swedish Drill, etc.
Military drill (for boys)."

The dilemma was the varied facilities that existed in the country at large. In trying to meet any demand for swimming from Leas and PES, there was not only the question of the facilities in, perhaps, one town, where swimming baths were unavailable, but where there was one (or more), it might not be in immediate reach of all schools. Even assuming that there were other locations like a river or pond within a city or town to meet the needs of all PES within an Lea area it is clear that an equality of facilities were not always available within that one locality, or indeed, comparatively with other Leas. Moreover, even in urban environments where swimming baths or places to swim were available for all children of an Lea within a relatively short distance of the schools, facilities for changing and dressing were an essential component of every school's desire to promote swimming on the curriculum. Not least safety precautions were essential. The possibilities for unequal facilities and resources were endless.

If the urban situation was problematical, then it was almost impossible in the rural context. It is true that these environments might have had access to more rivers, lakes and ponds where swimming might have been undertaken. In this respect, there was plenty of advice from ancient texts on how these kinds of facilities might be used. However, not only had the health and safety aspects of the children to be considered in the rural context but the question of travel to and from these locations was a very important element for consideration in any decision to provide swimming on the curriculum for children within the boundaries of any Lea.

Indeed, travel was one of those considerations which was always applicable to both urban and rural locations. Trains were the main means of travel but trains took time as well as having to be paid for by the Lea, school or children. Expenditure was thus a crucial element in any decision to undertake swimming lessons as part of the PES curriculum, not only payment for the facility but also for any travel arrangements, which might be necessary. The importance of this was the role of the District Auditor who was responsible to the LGB, which, in turn, was responsible for making sure that PES expenditure was legal and could not in any way be construed as *ultra vires*.

A further factor was the qualifications necessary for teachers to undertake instruction in swimming. Expenditure was a necessary concomitant in this regard, too, but even more crucial was the fact that there were very few women teachers who were capable of teaching swimming to girls, so that, in its early stages, at least, swimming was basically the preserve of boys in most cases.

For all those reasons, the Board was bound to make regulations concerning the approval of swimming instruction by schools. The most important of these was that approval had to be sanctioned by the local HMI. He could only sanction swimming as part of a specific and timetabled lesson declared as part of the curriculum of a particular school.

Nevertheless, wherever swimming took place in a locality, the time it took to travel to the appropriate facility plus the actual time for instruction was clearly an essential factor for its inclusion in the curriculum. The Board, therefore, executed an astute ploy in the development of swimming in the PES by allowing an extension of the school day into the evenings provided that swimming was designated as a subject of a school's curriculum and entered on the school's timetable. In that respect, the time taken for swimming could be construed as an attendance and properly paid for by an Lea.

The enquiry of the Cornwall Education Committee (*see* note 45 Introduction) and the subsequent reply of the Board, which refused the inclusion of swimming as part of a Physical Training curriculum as approved by circular 515, was another factor which had to be taken into account by both schools and Leas. That decision reinforced swimming as a separate curriculum subject under a proper timetabled instructor for a time, but was no doubt entirely unhelpful relative to those schools that were built some distance from a necessary facility and considered swimming as an educative physical exercise. The reason why the Board took this view is, perhaps, speculative, but was probably due to the fact that the Board had issued circular 515, which directed the attention of Leas and School managers to the criticisms noted in the *Inter-Departmental Committee on the Model Course of Physical Exercises*. The essence of the circular was that an emphasis should be placed on physical exercises outlined in the 1904 Syllabus, which did not rule out the influence of "football and cricket clubs (or in the case of girls, hockey clubs)", but made no mention of swimming and was a consequence of the concerns for the physical well-being of army recruits in the wake of the inadequacies of the physical state of army recruitment for the Boer War, which had been highlighted by the *Report of the Royal Commission on Physical Training (Scotland)*, 1903, and the 1904 Report.[3] The 1904 Syllabus replaced the Model Course, which had attracted the ire of a number of sources for being too militaristic in character, and, was the first attempt to address the concerns of the physical well-being of children in the light of the deficiencies experienced in army recruitment for the Boer War.

As it was, therefore, although it could be said that swimming was never permanently excluded from the curriculum after 1894, provided it was timetabled as a curriculum subject in its own right and approved by the local HMI, it wasn't until 1907, when the regulations concerning its inclusion as part of a general scheme of physical exercises were relaxed, that swimming could be considered in that context. Nevertheless, the wording of the regulation was, to say the least, ambivalent:

> " 2 (9)...In any course of Physical Exercises the general physical development of the scholar should be aimed at, and as a rule the official syllabus of physical training should be followed (i.e. 1904 Syllabus). The scholars of any school not situated wholly on a ground floor should be practiced in a fire drill. Instruction in Swimming may also be included in the Time Table."[4]

The reasons for schools to undertake swimming were obvious. More than 3,000 lives were lost on average annually in England and Wales by drowning.[5]

There are many examples of Leas wishing to include swimming in the curriculum. At a special meeting of the Lowestoft Education Committee, it was agreed to hire the Kirkley Baths at a charge of £1-2-6 (£1.12½p) for 100 scholars.[6] Similarly Southport Education Committee agreed that the School Timetable should be so planned that boys from Standards V, VI and VII could attend the Corporation Swimming Baths one day per week. Each class was taken to the baths by a teacher responsible for the children's safety.[7] Bristol Education Committee was also successful in promoting swimming. Of 2,711 children in weekly attendance, 1,220 learned to swim, 131 passed the test of rescuing the drowning; 858 children gained the Committee's certificate and 362 learned to swim the width of the bath. Those unable to swim more than ten yards were classed as non-swimmers. The number of girls learning to swim was 252, boys 968.[8]

The problem of teachers who were unable to swim was dealt with by the Bath Education Committee in the following manner. It delayed the instruction of children until additional accommodation was available. The delay was useful in the sense that volunteer teachers were able to attend classes by themselves to receive instruction in swimming. Proposals were based on the assumption that charges for the teachers' class would be 5d for men and 3½d for women and a 5/- (25p) per head charge as a tuition fee for a course of lessons and that cost was defrayed by the authority.[9]

In 1905, Kingston upon Hull Education Committee first placed swimming on the curriculum of the elementary schools. The committee appointed Miss L Shannon, holder of the Royal Life Saving Society (RLSS) medallion and instructor's certificate. She taught swimming and various methods of life-saving for which she held the RLSS certificate. Of the 800 girls she taught in the previous year 580 learned to swim. The most advanced girls were from the Daltry Street School who swam a length of the Madeley Street Baths. At the end of the season the Education committee intended to give certificates to boys and girls on the following basis:

1. a first-class certificate was awarded for swimming 220 yards in any stroke in six minutes plus three strokes of sixty yards in the following styles; breast, overarm and trudgeon* and a dive from a height of six feet
2. a second-class certificate was awarded for swimming 100 yards in two minutes twenty-five seconds plus forty yards on the back and a dive from a height of four feet
3   a third-class certificate was awarded for swimming twenty yards breast stroke, twenty yards back stroke and a dive from the wall of the bath.[10]

*Quote: There is a prevalent idea that the double over-arm and the Trudgen strokes are the same, but that is a mistake. The stroke that J Trudgen brought back with him from Buenos Ayres was carried out without any roll, the head being held well up and erect; the arms were used alternately in rather short strokes, and the leg kick was that of the ordinary breast stroke – one leg kick to every second stroke with the arms. It is common knowledge now (vide Badminton and Ralph Thomas) that this stroke, or one like it, was swum by the Assyrians over two thousand years ago, although when Trudgen first used it in England and he caused quite a stir among swimmers.[11] (Note: Badminton is a reference to the Badminton Library series.[12])

Birmingham Education Committee held a gigantic swimming carnival on Tuesday 18 September 1906 for the allocation of free passes for schoolboys who were able to swim a length of the bath. Of the total numbers who swam, there were 753 renewals and 1,270 free passes.[13]

In spite of these numerous examples of swimming in the PES around the country, Northamptonshire County Council wrote to the Board on 14 January 1907 concerning a contribution of £5-5-0 to a UDC within their boundaries for the purpose of swimming out of school hours. By then the Board had decided on the precedent of approval by the HMI and shown on the Timetable of the school, irrespective of the time of day, and, therefore, could be attributed to the ordinary school curriculum by article 44 of the code. The instruction could, therefore, be recognised by the Board. Nevertheless, the Board could offer no advice on the expenditure of the Lea which was a matter for the District Auditor except to say that if the instruction was approved by the HMI and timetabled as a curriculum subject, then any expense in respect of the of that approval could properly be included in the expenditure required for maintaining the school.[14]

A further and separate letter from the Borough of New Windsor asked what qualifications were needed for an instructor in swimming to have to teach swimming in the ordinary school hours. Repeating the familiar mantra about the timetable, the Board, nevertheless, did not require any particular qualifications to be possessed by a teacher to teach swimming, but assumed that the Lea would satisfy itself that the teacher appointed was properly qualified for the post.[15]

Until the middle of 1910, the grounds for swimming in the PES were basically considered on educational grounds as illustrated above. A letter from Cheshire County Council,[16] however, changed this rationale somewhat on both medical and educational grounds. A letter[17] dated 19 September 1910 from the Board stated categorically

(a)   that a teacher was always to be present at any instruction
(b)   the number of children was limited to 20 unless the teacher accompanying the class was also a competent instructor in swimming in which case a maximum number of children was allowed to be but limited to 30.
(c)   The children should be examined by the School Medical Officer (SMO) prior to their admission to the class although Selby-Bigge offered caution in this regard as not always being a practicable consideration.

Further observations were made to Northamptonshire County Council regarding children swimming instruction at Earls Barton near the River Nene.[18] Eventually, Mr Holland, secretary to the Northamptonshire Education Committee and Dr Mason, Assistant Medical

Officer (MO), met George Newman on 19 May 2011. In the end Mr Walrond[19] agreed that the scheme could go ahead provided the boys volunteered for the lessons; that no ill-nourished or unfit boys attended; that the boys were to be accompanied by a master and that the boys were required to attend the first two of the forty-minute afternoon lessons before their departure for the swimming instruction.

In one sense, therefore, although the Board's approach to swimming was clear, it confused many Leas, not least because of the overarching role of the LGB.

The records of the Surrey Education Committee, however, show a gradual increase in the implementation of swimming as a curriculum subject except as far as the problem of availability of swimming places and teachers qualified to teach the subject within the county's boundaries are concerned. This state of affairs was undoubtedly due to three factors:

1. The enthusiasm, in the first instance, of Major Norman who initiated a swimming programme for the PES. Major Norman was clearly appointed to implement the 1904 Syllabus, which made no reference at all to swimming and was largely a construct of physical exercises based on the Swedish system of physical training, with some acknowledgment to the role of games in the physical education curriculum. After Major Norman's initial work, Captain Mignon was to carry on the good work of his predecessor. In, at least some respects, some revision of the

   "effect of the army influence on school work was unfortunate in several respects.....Officers never actually took a class (in drill)"[20]

   In Surrey, in drill, they certainly gave instruction to both teachers' classes and children on inspection while both were deeply involved in the organisation of swimming in the PES, which progressively increased.

2. The enthusiastic support of the SEC in its acceptance of circular 515 and the dual appointments of Major Norman and Dr Thomas Henry Jones.

3. The support of the parents, children and teachers in the PES which appear to show a gradual acceptance of swimming as a curriculum subject worthy of note in spite of the fact that swimming took place in all sorts of backwaters, as well as Swimming Baths, where these were available and within easy reach of the school. The SEC minutes do not mention the number of children who were refused swimming by their parents or who could not swim on the grounds of disablement or ill-health but the statistics revealed by the minutes would suggest that these were insubstantial.

The First World War interrupted the status quo of physical education generally but of the three leaders who had led the subject at various stages of the subject's development in the PES of the County of Surrey, Major Norman, Captain Mignon and Miss Dorothy Le Couteur, it might be said that they all contributed immensely to the physical development of the children in the schools. They did so with dedication, understanding and a coherent knowledge and application of the subject's basic principles based on the wisdom of the times and the regulatory control of the Board of Education.

50

Notes

1. PP XXV, 1886: PP XXIX+XXX, 1887: PP XXXV-XXXVII, 1888; *Reports of the Royal Commission to enquire into the working of the Elementary Education Acts*, (Cross Commission) 1886-1888.

2. Education Department, *Code of Regulations for day Schools with Schedules and Appendices*, 1894, HMSO.

3. PP Volume XXX, 1, Command 1507, *Report of the Royal Commission on Physical Training (Scotland)*, Volume 1 Report and Appendix, 1903.
    PP Volume XXX,Command 1508, *Report of the Royal Commission on Physical training (Scotland)*, Volume II Minutes of Evidence and Index, 1903.
    PP Volume XXXII, Command 2175, *Report of the Inter-Departmental Committee on Physical Deterioration*, Volume I Report and Appendix, 1904.
    PP Volume XXXII, Command 2210, *Minutes of Evidence taken before the Inter-Departmental Committee on Physical Deterioration*, Volume II List of Witnesses and Minutes of Evidence, 1904

4. Board of Education, *Code of Regulations for Public Elementary Schools in England with Schedules*, 3, 2-9, HMSO 1907.

5. *Hansard*, 4th Series, Volume 140, 10 August to 15 August 1904, 11 August 1904, column 219.

6. *The Schoolmaster*, 2 July 1904, 15.

7. ibid., 9 July 1904, 80.

8. ibid., 3 December 1904, 1102.

9. ibid., 8 April 1905, 706.

10. *The (Hull) Daily Mail*, 13 June 1906, 3.

11. Sachs, Frank. *The Complete Swimmer*, 144, Methuen & Co Ltd., London, 1912.

12. Sinclair, Archibald and Henry, William. *Swimming*, 86-89, Longmans, Green, and Co., London, The Badminton Library, 2nd Edition, 1894.

13. *The Schoolmaster*, 22 September 1906, 500.

14. TNA, Ed. 111/117, Northamptonshire County Council letter, 14 January 1907.

15. TNA, Ed 19/7, Borough of New Windsor, 6 June 1907, letter 12131 B.

16. TNA, Ed 125/21, Cheshire County Council, 4 July 1910, letter.

17. ibid., Board of Education letter, 19 September 1910.

18. TNA, Ed 19/192, Nortamptonshire County Council, 17 July 1909, letter 14731B. Board of Education letter, 31 July 1909. 09?4731 B.

19. ibid., Board of Education letter, 10 June 1911, 11/13005 B. (In 1911, T R Walrond was an Assistant Secretary at the Board of Education).

20. McIntosh, Peter C. *Physical Education in England Since 1800*, 149, Revised & Enlarged Edition, Bell & Hyman, London, 1968.

APPENDIX I
THE FULL TEXT OF THE LETTER ON THE ART OF
SWIMMING AND LIFE SAVING (SURREY)
Source: *The Advertiser* (*The Dorking Advertiser*) 14 May 1896, 5.

The following letter, signed, among others, by W S Hankins, Polytechnic Swimming Club (SC), M Laurie, Magpie SC, James Freeman, London Schools Swimming Association, William Henry, Honorary Secretary Life-Saving Society, FW Ashton, Grenfell SC, Duncan Black, Life-Saving Society, has been sent to the press:-

> We would respectfully venture to direct your attention and solicit your practical help in the promotion of the knowledge of the art of swimming and life-saving. It is quite unnecessary for us to point out the value of such knowledge, either from the health-promoting or humane points of view, as both are almost universally admitted.
>
> The main questions which concern us are:-
>
> 1. How best to bring this subject prominently before the people; and (2) how to stimulate public opinion in favour of its general adoption as a branch of instruction in schools, colleges, and other educational institutions.
>
> Much good has undoubtedly been done of late years by the hundreds of swimming organisations in this country and in the colonies to bring about these much-to-be-desired results, but as the work in which these institutions have been engaged (unlike football and other land games) has to a great extent been left unnoticed by the Press generally, their work, in our opinion, has not proved such a power for good or made such speedy progress as it might, were some notice was taken of the efforts put forth.
>
> The games of football, etc., owe much to the Press for the position they now occupy in public favour, and we see no reason why the art of swimming should not be equally favoured, especially when one remembers its usefulness, and how many lives might be saved out of the thousands that are annually lost by drowning.
>
> The neglect of this subject is in great measure due to parents and scholastic authorities who do not consider it to be their duty to teach the children this useful knowledge, but we think that with the aid of the Press improvement would soon follow, and if only a small proportion of encouragement was given to existing

organisations which promote that valuable art as compared with other pastimes, we should rapidly approach the ideal when swimming and life-saving would become so well recognised that it would soon form part of our national education.

That the subject to which you we invite your attention may receive your favourable consideration and valuable support is our earnest wish.

APPENDIX II
SWIMMING AND WASHING VERMINOUS CHILDREN
IN THE LONDON SCHOOL BOARD

Source: *Report of the Physical Education Sub-Committee on Bathing
Accommodation & Swimming Classes (Public Elementary Schools) with Appendices*

*Please note that the reference to the "Board" in this appendix refers exclusively to the London School Board.

In May 1890 the *Physical Education Sub-Committee on Bathing Accommodation and Swimming Classes*[1] of the London School Board reported (1890 Report) that the New Education Code recently published contained the following:

12. "An attendance means attendance at secular instruction"
    "(f) In making up the minimum time constituting an attendance there may be reckoned time occupied by instruction in any of the following subjects, whether or not it is given in the school premises by the ordinary teachers of the school, provided that special and appropriate provision, approved by an inspector, is made for such instruction, and the times for giving it are entered in the approved Time Table:-

Drawing	Manual Instruction
Science	Suitable Physical Exercises
Military Drill (for boys)	Practical Cookery or Laundry Work (for Girls above Standard III)"

It is clear that this regulation basically remained the basis of the future regulatory codes concerning physical exercises in the PES, including that of 1894 (note 2, the conclusion), and gives examples of what activities might be construed as suitable physical exercises, i.e. swimming, gymnastics and Swedish Drill. It is interesting to note that "Military drill for boys" was separated from this main regulatory injunction.

The Sub-committee in 1890 wasn't at all impressed with the 1890 code.

Its criticism lay in the notion that there could hardly be a more suitable physical exercise than that of swimming and it was not for the HMI to determine the question of what was a suitable physical exercise. It would have been far more sensible, the Report opined, for the 1890 code to have clearly stated that instruction in swimming was included as a suitable physical exercise. Although the Education Department met this criticism with the 1894 code, it retained that element of requiring approval by the HMI, and, as previously suggested, this was basically because of the variable conditions that pertained throughout the country as a whole.

The Sub-committee, however, unable to foresee future regulations, observed that until swimming was definitely recognised by the Education Department, and, was adapted by the School Board, *an attempt should be made by voluntary effort* (author's italics) to secure for the children in all PES the great benefit of being able to swim. The Sub-committee, therefore, recommended:

1. That the Board memorialize the Education Department to make provision in the New Code for the inclusion of instruction in swimming on similar terms to those now presented for Military Drill by the addition of the words "including instruction in swimming" after the words "suitable physical exercises" in clause 12, sub clause (f)

2. That a copy of this Report be sent to each Local Authority and that they be asked to grant facilities for the use of baths at a cheap rate by the children of the PES.

3. That a copy of this Report be sent to the Chairman of each group of Managers of the Board's Schools, to each Head Teacher in the service of the Board and to such other persons of whom the committee have knowledge, as are interested in the promotion of swimming and that their aid be asked in the promotion of swimming classes in the schools.

4. That the London County Council (LCC) be asked to promote a more general establishment of public swimming baths for the benefit of the inhabitants of London and their children.

5. That a copy of this Report be sent to each Member of Parliament representing a London constituency and to each member of the LCC.

This 1890 Report, therefore, may, in one sense, be said to have been an open invitation for voluntary activity in swimming to proceed within the confines of the London School Board's PES.

The Sub-committee commenced their present enquiry by sending a circular (Sub-Appendix B) with questions to various Vestries, District Boards and Proprietors of Bathing establishments in the following terms:

1. What was the existing bathing accommodation in your Parish, District or Establishment?

2. On what terms and under what conditions was such accommodation made available for the use of children attending PES in particular with regard to price, the hours, the number of bathers, the supply of towels and the provision for the teaching of swimming.

3. What suggestions could be made by which the Board could cooperate with local Bathing Authorities or Associations, or could encourage the establishment of swimming classes?

The Sub-committee also addressed to the officials of the Board asking them to furnish the Sub-committee with as full particulars as possible of any voluntary effort to establish , in their several Divisions, swimming classes in connection with PES of London. (Sub-Appendix C)

Indeed, in 1893 the formation of the LSSA was due to London Board School Headmasters, was controlled by them, and, they were responsible for the teaching of swimming and life-saving. The decision to form the LSSA was taken at Victoria Park Lake in Mile End. JE Gardner was the first honorary secretary and it was due to his powers of organisation that the foundations of the LSSA were formed and it was due to his efforts that its subsequent success was based. As in Surrey, swimming and life-saving was not on the timetable of schools, but it is clear from the 1890 Report that the Sub-committee was extremely supportive of swimming and although there were obstacles to overcome, such as the training of teachers, nevertheless it was a momentous process to establish the LSSA with so much success so quickly.[2]

One reason why this success was established so quickly, may have come about, in part, due to a deputation that the Sub-committee received from the Amateur Swimming Association (ASA). In essence, the ASA submitted a scheme addressed to the Chairman of the Committee on Physical Education for the London School Board.

"Sir,

We, the undersigned members of the deputation appointed by the Executive Committee of the ASA.....have based this draft scheme on voluntary support from the general public.

Scheme

1. Establish a subscription fund under the auspices of the Board. The Board would make itself responsible for the equitable distribution of the fund.
2. Obtain terms from both proprietors and public baths for special tickets of admission between certain times on certain days.
3. Establish a local centre at each bath for the neighbouring schools, each centre to be managed by a Committee comprising 1 or more representatives from the staff and manage of each school, to make local arrangements, apply grants received from the Central Committee and secure the services of honorary instructors.
4. The fund to be distributed under the direction of the Board by a Central Committee.
   (a) One portion, say two-fifths, to be divided among the local centres, to form the nuclei of their own prize funds.
   (b) One portion, say two-fifths to be granted to local centres in poor districts to be used exclusively for the purchase of tickets, for children who cannot afford to pay for their own admission.
   (c) The remainder, say one-fifth, to meet general expenses, and to provide prizes for a general swimming meeting to be held under the direction of the Board as the Drill competition is at present.

The ASA will be pleased to arrange for gratuitous instruction to the schoolmasters in the Board's employ, who may desire it, at any swimming baths in London, and can assure your Committee of the cordial support and assistance of all the London Swimming Clubs."

(signed) W Henry, Zephyr Swimming Club

GH Payne, Nautilus Swimming Club

HF Mawbey, St James's Swimming Club

Edward J Tackley, Hon. Sec. St James's SC.

The LSSA was not, however, the first voluntary organisation to attempt to form an association in swimming for the children of the PES in London.

The 1890 Report came about because the School Management Committee of the London School Board referred a resolution of 29 March 1889 to the Physical Education Sub-committee. The resolution had been moved by Edric Bayley and seconded by Sir Edmund Hay Currie. That resolution resolved:

> "That it be referred to the Sub-committee on Physical Education to enquire into present bathing accommodation provided by the local authorities in the different School Board Divisions of London and into the very best means which by which the Board can cooperate with such authorities and with Voluntary Associations and can otherwise give facilities for the establishment of swimming classes for boys and girls in connection with the PES of London and to report to this committee"

The Sub-committee briefly recapitulated the substance of a report submitted by the Works Committee to the Board on 26 June 1872 (Sub-Appendix A).

That Report was submitted by the Works Committee because they were instructed on the 11 October 1871 to consider and report upon the following referral from the Board:

Resolved on the motion of John MacGregor and seconded by Robert Freeman:

> "That to facilitate bathing and swimming as part of the education of children in the PES, it is desirable to promote concerted action between public bodies and others who can provide Swimming Baths accessible to large numbers at a small charge.
>
> That the Works and General Purposes Committee be requested to enquire as to the present bathing accommodation in the school districts and the best means suggested for its systematic extension; and to report thereon, so as to allow due time for the provision of cheap and convenient Swimming baths for the next bathing season."

The results of the enquiries were not of a very encouraging character; most of the Bath Companies or proprietors declined to agree to an exclusive use of the baths by schoolchildren; only three proposed distinct terms for such children and in only one case was a bath offered for their exclusive use, at a convenient hour for the payment of 1d. With this exception, the usual customers appear to be "numerous enough to prevent Managers from lowering the tariff by special arrangement, at all events during the most crowded season."

The Committee suggested that bathing tickets might be given to children as rewards for good conduct at school and thought that if the expenses could not "legally be borne by the School Fund, the School Managers might, at any rate, make the arrangements by which the cost to bathers might be reduced". The Sub-committee, having ascertained that the Board had no power to legally expend money on the construction of swimming baths, could "only recommend that the Managers of Board Schools should be urged to give all reasonable encouragement to those children who desire to bathe and learn to swim".

On this Report the Board adopted the following resolution on the 26 June 1872:

"That in accordance with the recommendation of the Report, the Managers of Board Schools be urged to give all reasonable encouragement to those children who desire to bathe and to learn how to swim."

The Board subsequently addressed a letter to the Education Department with reference to the insertion of a clause in the Elementary Education Act, 1873, (1873 Act) giving power to School Boards " to expend money, either in providing Swimming Baths themselves for the children in Board Schools, or in making payment for such children in any Public Baths already existing."

The 1873 Act did not give the required powers.

However, in 1875 an association called the *London Schools Swimming Club* was formed. This club had as its aim the encouragement of swimming, for both boys and girls, by the fostering of clubs, the obtaining of permission to use lakes in the various parks, the receiving of subscriptions, the making of advantageous arrangements with the Commissioners and Bath proprietors, etc., the organisation of a system of voluntary instruction by Board School Teachers and by the award of prizes to both instructors and children.

The Club, under the energetic direction of its honorary secretaries did some excellent work and continued in existence until 1884. When subscriptions, however, did not adequately meet expenses, it became inactive.

In 1887, the late Charles R White, former member of the Board, feeling that something should be done to save so useful an institution from extinction offered to the Board, a Silver Challenge Cup (valued at about thirty guineas [i.e. £30 and 30 shillings = £31-10-0]) to be competed for by children from both Board and Non-Board Schools. Nevertheless, the club again lapsed into a quiescent state.

On 17 November 1887, the Board determined on a motion of Mr Bousfield to appoint a Special Committee:

"to consider the present subjects and modes of instruction in the Board Schools and to report whether such changes can be made as shall secure that children leaving school shall be more fitted than they are now the duties and work of life before them."

The Special Committee reported that there were forty-three Boys' Schools and forty-eight Girls' Schools where no drill was taken.....play, to be effective for physical improvement must be organised for the children by others. "It recommended that playgrounds attached to schools be used for the formation of clubs for hardy sports, gymnastic exercises and drill and that the school organisation be used for the establishment of field sports and swimming classes."

The Special committee further recommended:

"That the Chairman of the Board be asked to convene a meeting of Local Managers and others to consider the question of organized physical education out of school hours and to request personal help in this work."

The Report of the Special Committee on the subjects and modes of instruction in the Board Schools was received by the Board and the above recommendations were adopted on 1 November 1888 when about eighty Representative Managers attended and the following resolutions were passed unanimously:

"(a)   That the Resolution of the Board, with reference to Physical Training, meets with the hearty approval of Local Managers; and that this meeting of Local Managers pledges itself to urge upon the Managers and Teachers under the Board the importance of giving especial attention to every effort to promote the physical training of children in the schools.

(b)   That in the opinion of this meeting, it is desirable that the Chairman of each group of schools should bring the question of organizing Physical Education out of school hours before the Teachers and Managers of the Group of Schools over which he presides: that the Managers of neighbouring schools not under the Board, should be invited where possible, to submit their views; and that in due course, a Report be made to the Board of the action taken in connection with this Resolution."

In accordance with the Resolution of the Board 6 December 1888, a circular letter containing copies of the above Resolution of the Special Committee on the subjects and modes of instruction in the Board's schools, and, of the Resolution of the meeting of 29 November 1888, was sent to the Chairman of each Group of Managers of Board Schools, asking him to enter into communication with the Managers of the neighbouring elementary schools, not under the Board, and to submit a report upon the question of organised physical education out of school hours to the Clerk of the Board.

Very few replies were received relative to this circular, (probably) from want of some outline of a scheme on the subject upon which they could make suggestions. One difficulty that had been pointed out was the fact that few teachers lived in the immediate neighbourhoods of their schools, and they were naturally glad after school hours to get to their homes and to where they found their friends and their means of recreation.

On 9 May 1889 the Board resolved:

"That the School Management Committee and the Evening Classes Committee be authorised to wait upon the Vice-President of the Committee of Council on Education – i.e. the Education Department – and to submit the following Memorial containing suggestions with reference to the New Code."

A Memorial was, therefore, submitted by the Board to the Education Department and requested modifications to the code of 1889, which had been laid before the Houses of Parliament.

The first amendment the Board requested was to Article 12 which read:

" An attendance means an attendance at secular instruction."

12(f) For boys military drill under a competent instructor, for not more than 2 hours in any week or 40 hours in any school year, and for girls, lessons in practical cookery, where the inspector reports that special and appropriate provision is made for teaching it, for not more than 40 hours in any school year, are reckoned as instruction for the purposes of this Article. Scholars of any PES may attend science classes held at any place approved by the Inspector."

The modifications to this Article that the Board requested were in six parts:

"(i)   After the words 'military drill' to insert or other suitable physical exercises.

(ii)   After the words 'for girls' to insert 'suitable physical exercises and'

(iii) That the words 'may attend science classes' the following words be substituted 'May attend science or manual training classes, or classes in any subjects recognised by the Department of Science and Art'.

(iv)   That in the case of Infants' Schools, there be provision for a proper variety of physical exercises and occupations

(v)   That the attendance for cookery be for not more than 3 hours in any week, nor for more than 60 hours in any school year

(vi)   That physical education may include, not only military drill, but gymnastics, swimming and other exercises approved by the Education Department as beneficial to the health of children."

The second alteration that the Board sought was related to Section 20 of The Elementary Education Act, 1876, which concerned the income of schools and required the insertion of 'physical education, manual instruction and modelling' be inserted after the word 'cooking' in the 1889 code.

The third modification concerned Article 96 (b) of the code. It read:

"A merit grant of 2/-, 4/- or 6/-, if the Inspector reports the school or class to be fair, good or excellent allowing for the special circumstances of the case and having regard to the provision made for

(1)   suitable instruction in the elementary subjects

(2)   simple lessons on objects and on the phenomena of nature and of common life and

(3)   appropriate and varied occupations"

The Board suggested that the words "and physical exercises" be inserted after the words "elementary subjects".

The Memorial was sent to the Education Department who declined to receive a deputation on the subject. Nevertheless, it is discernible that that part of the 1890 code relating to physical exercises, and, is quoted at the beginning of this Appendix, shows some movement to the London Board's point of view. Similarly, the 1894 code shows even more. The general consensus of opinion on these changes has been ascribed to the Cross Commission's three Reports,[3] and, it is indeed, difficult to exclude their influence, nevertheless, the School Board for London was equally influential in these changes especially as they had introduced the Swedish System of Drill for the girls attending London's PES in 1878.[4]

On 4 July 1889 the Board had before them the following remarks of HMI, made on a Government Report, with reference to the Girls' Department of Orange Street School in the Borough of Southwark:

"Some of the children are still sadly dirty. Years ago I recommended that means should be found for washing their persons and freeing their clothes from vermin. In a similar school, the Birmingham School Board is setting up a bath – a most beneficial measure not yet tried in London."

Subsequently, on the recommendation of the School Management Committee, the Board decided to ask the Education Department whether, if the Board act upon the advice of

HMI, the Department would be prepared to sanction a loan for a bath to be erected at Orange Street School or the neighbouring school of Pocock Street.

On 15 July 1889, the Education Department replied stating that their Lordships would be unable to assent to a loan for the provision of a bath as proposed in the Board's letter of the 9 July 1889 at either Orange Street or Pocock Street Schools under Section 10 of the 1873 Act.

The School Management Committee made enquiries on the subject from the Liverpool and Bristol School Boards.

The Liverpool School Board replied in the following terms. A plunge bath was provided in all but the first seven or eight schools erected by the Board. The provision was made in the plans submitted to the Education Department. The cost was included in the original tenders and defrayed from the loans granted for the erection of the schools. There was no cost of maintenance other than the charge for water and this did not appear as a separate sum but was included in the water rent. The attention of the auditor had not been especially called to the subject and consequently the Liverpool School Board was unable to say what view the auditor had taken regarding the legality of the expenditure.

The Bristol School Board replied that the entire cost of construction attached to the Castle School was paid out of the School Fund through the current account. The cost of maintenance was also defrayed out of the School Fund. The auditor had passed the accounts from time to time without taking any exception to the expenditure.

On 11 November 1889 the Board addressed a further letter to the Education Department pointing out that it was extremely desirable that means should be provided to give effect to the suggestion of HMI with regard to the Orange Street School and asking that the matter might be favourably reconsidered.

On 14 December 1889 the Education Department replied stating that the Birmingham School Board had not provided a swimming bath by means of a loan and adding that their Lordships had been advised by the Law Officers of the Crown that they had no power to sanction a loan for such an object.

A reference to this decision was made in the *School Board Chronicle* of 26 October 1889 offering an explanation of this decision by the Education Department in respect of the Aston Manor (Birmingham) School Board. The Sites and Buildings Committee had reported that they had invited tenders for the erection of a swimming bath in connection with one of the schools that the Board was enlarging. The committee recommended that a tender amounting to £550 be accepted for the purpose. The chairman in course of a speech in support of the recommendation said that from enquiries made, he had found that the Education Department was opposed to the establishment of baths. In Bristol two of the Board Schools had baths attached and he had been told that each bath did not cost more than £15 per annum. He could see no objection to a small charge being made for the use of the bath – say a ½d or a ¼d per child. Subsequently the recommendation was adopted six to four.

Sub-Appendix D gives particulars of the provision made for public bathing in London. In sixteen parishes one or more swimming baths were provided under the Public Baths and Washhouses Acts. Three of these parishes, Lewisham, St Pancras and St George's, Hanover square had two establishments. The total number of Public Swimming Baths was forty-one. There were twenty-five private bath establishments with thirty-six swimming baths. The price charged for school children varied from a penny to three pence (thruppence or 3d) and in some cases included towels and bathing dress. As many as eight public and five private baths admit children at 1d.

Meanwhile, the Board was obviously active in pursuing its desire to come to a positive conclusion to the request it had made to the Education Department concerning the Orange Board School.

On 10 October 1889 it had received and adopted the following Report and Recommendation of the Works Committee:

"That the committee have had under consideration letters from the Headmaster of the 'Pulteney School', Berwick Street, Soho, (Westminster Division) stating that the Honourable Dudley Campbell (late manager of this school) has offered to defray the expense of the purchase and fitting up of three spray baths (Bartholomew's patent) for the thorough periodical washing of such children as require it; and that the Managers were unanimous in accepting the offer; pointing out that there is great need for such baths in connection with some of the children attending the school; stating that the teachers will superintend the washing of the children as part of the school routine, no service being required of the schoolkeeper; and asking permission to have these baths fixed for the school.

The committee have ascertained that there is a suitable position in which these baths might be placed, and have obtained an estimate from a local firm of the cost of providing 60 baths per day, on the above system, particulars of which are set out below:-

No. of boys to be bathed everyday - 60	No. of baths to be filled up - 3
Water used for 60 baths per day - 180	Cost at 1/6 per 1000 gallons - 4d
Gas - 75 feet	Cost (2/6 per 1000 feet) - 2d

Allowing a margin for gas and water over this estimate, which could only be correct under discipline, say

Water cost per day	4½d
Gas	3 d
Total cost per day	7½d
Cost per week	3s-1½d

The Committee are of the opinion that it would be desirable that the expenditure should be tried, and that the offer of the Honourable Dudley Campbell should be accepted, the Board being, of course, responsible for the supply of the necessary gas and water. They accordingly recommended:

'That the thanks of the Board be given to the Honourable D. Campbell for his offer to defray the expense of purchasing and filling up 3 spray baths in connection with the Pulteney School, Berwick Street, Soho, (Westminster Division) as described in the Report and that the offer be accepted.'"

Sub-Appendix A attached to the Report
Report submitted to the Board by the Works Committee on the 26 June 1872.

The Works Committee were instructed on the 11 October 1871 to consider and Report upon the following reference from the Board:-

Resolved on the motion of John MacGregor seconded by Robert Freeman:

"That to facilitate bathing and swimming as part of the education of children in PES, it is desirable to promote concerted action between public bodies and others who can provide Swimming Baths accessible to large numbers at a small charge.

That the Works and General Purposes be requested to enquire as to the present bathing accommodation the schools districts and the best means suggested for its systematic extension; and to report thereon so as to allow due time for the provision of cheap and convenient Swimming baths for the next bathing season."

From information obtained by the Committee there were about twenty-five separate establishments in the Metropolitan Districts, which provided swimming bath accommodation. The area of the baths amounted to nearly 50,000 sq. feet, which allowed about 1,000 people bathing in them at the same time. The price charged for each bather going separately varied from 2d to 1/- inclusive of the use of towels.

Many of the baths were of a small superficial area; some were in localities not readily accessible to the poorer classes. Most of them, when open in the cold season of the year, were warmed, and this practice is in some cases carried on to an injurious extent, especially for such bathers were encouraged to remain long in the water. On the other hand, bathers who were ill-fed were not always able to endure a cold bath.

Circulars were addressed from the Board to each of the Bath Companies or Proprietors, requesting terms for special arrangements for the bathing of School Board children and replies were received from thirteen establishments. Only three proposed distinct terms.

Some of the Bath managers were hindered by their Bye-laws from making any reduction in their fees. Others noted difficulties admitting children at inconvenient hours. Several of the managers were not prepared to provide towels. Most of them declined to agree to an exclusive use of the swimming bath by children from schools.

The accommodation on the platform of these thirteen baths was an average at the rate of one bather for each twenty feet of bath area. The use of a plunge bath for an hour, or even two hours at a time was not uncommon among the ordinary second class bathers. The discipline that the school managers could enforce would prevent this inordinate excess, and so, would at least, double the available accommodation when it was used methodically.

The following were the cases in which the most favourable terms were prepared by the Managers for the use of swimming baths by School Board children under discipline and by special agreement.

The Greenwich Baths were prepared to grant exclusive use from 8 to 12 o'clock three days weekly, sixty bathers at a time at a cost of ½d each bather. Towels would cost ½d each bather and reckoning the time accepted as a quarter of an hour, about 900 children could bathe there daily at an expense of 1d each.

St Giles's Baths said they would charge £1 for 140 tickets or about ½d each (*sic*) without towels and without exclusive use. (Tickets at ½d each at a cost of £1 overall would amount to 480 tickets).

Tower Hamlets would charge £2 for 500 bathers, about 1d each, and towels at a cost of 1/- per score or ½d each. Although this bath had a large area ordinary customers would also claim simultaneous use.

Wenlock Baths in Wenlock Road, City Road were large and 230 people could use the platform at once, the charge would be 1½d each and ½d for towels from 7-9am, during which time about 2,000 children could bathe at 2d each.

St Pancras Baths would allow seventy bathers at a time at 2d each including towels.

Poplar Baths propose similar terms.

From these data only the Baths at Greenwich appear available for exclusive use at a convenient hour and for the payment of 1d.

The Committee believed, however, that many children could learn to swim...if bathing tickets were given to them as rewards for good conduct at school. This comment is reminiscent of the 1894 code, which announced that after 31 August 1895, the higher grant of 1/6 for Discipline and Organisation would not be paid to any school in which provision was not made for the instruction of Swedish or other drill or suitable physical exercises. In other words, even in 1872, reward for good behaviour was the probability of a free swimming ticket.[5]

Bathing in the Serpentine and other park waters, and in the Thames and canals was very restricted by very stringent rules, which, when enforced, almost precluded any orderly or systematic use of such places by children who regularly attended school and in none of these cases were there convenient places for bathing decently in water reasonably clear and for dressing afterwards with any comfort.

The strong and natural desire of children who wished to bathe, especially in hot weather, and the manifest advantage – physically and morally – led to the proposal by members of the Board for a swimming bath to be built in one of the new school premises then being prepared by the Board.

Nevertheless, the solicitor of the Board informed the Board that, in his opinion, the Board had no power under the Act to expend money on the provision of a swimming bath; news which the committee learned with great regret.

Consequently, the Board could only recommend that the Managers of Board Schools should be urged to give all reasonable encouragement to those who desired to bathe and learn how to swim. Subsequently, a resolution based on these observations was adopted on 26 June 1872.

At a later date, on the recommendation of the School Management Committee, the Board addressed a letter to the Education Department in accordance with the terms of the following report:

" The Works Committee reported to the Board on the 26 June 1872 that the solicitor to the Board had advised the Board that the Board had no powers, under the Elementary Education Act, 1870, (1870 Act) to expend money either in providing swimming baths themselves for the children in the Board Schools, or in making payment for such children in any public baths already existing. As the School Management Committee think that this is a matter of great importance, they recommend that a letter be addressed to the Education Department requesting, that, in the Amending Act to be promoted in Parliament next year, 1873, the Department will introduce a clause giving power to School Boards for the above object."

No such action was taken by the Education Department in the 1873 Act, and it was, therefore, of no surprise that the London Swimming Club was formed in 1875 on a voluntary basis.

Sub-Appendix B-Selected Entries

Questions addressed to the various Vestries, District Boards and Proprietors of Bathing Establishments.
(see page 2/3)

Parish or District	What is the existing Public Bathing Accomodation in Your Parish, District or Establishment	On what terms & under what conditions can such accommodation be made available for the use of children attending PES in particular with regard to:						What Suggestions can you make by which the Board can cooperate with local Bathing Authorities or Associations or can encourage the establishment of swimming	Remarks
		Price	Hours	Number of bathers	Size of bath (ft)	Supply of towels to each bather	Provision for teaching swimming classes		
1	2	3	4	5	6	7	8	9	10
Battersea Latchmere Road	2 baths 1st & 2nd class	1st class 2nd class 100 tickets for 8/4 (10% free tickets to be given to poor children attending Board Schools	bath to be used at certain times	-	100 x 35 75 x 25	2 1	-	-	-
Bermondsey Spa-Road	ditto	1st class 2nd class 1½d	6-8am 12.15-1.30pm 4.30-6pm	150	80 x 30 80 x 30	1	-	that cooperation of the teachers be enlisted and notices posted in schools	every facility given to both sexes
Bethnal Green & St Matthew	ditto	1st class 100 tickets for £1 2nd class	Tues Weds Thurs	200	103 x 40 60 x 24	1 and bathing drawers	-	-	-
Greenwich Public Baths	ditto	1st class 2ndclass 2d each		accommodation limited	90 x 20 100 x 18				during favourable season no accommodation for school children
Hammersmith Black's Road	1	2d each if in charge of leader	7-10am on Sats only	80	-	children to bring their own	attendant would teach swimming for fee	masters and teachers should take more interest	-
Kensington Lancaster Road	3 1st, 2nd & 3rd + ladies bath	1st, 2nd & 3rd 3d each if accompanied by teacher	Tues and Thurs 5-8pm	-	61 x 25	-	-	-	pupil teachers admitted upon some terms between 5-8pm on Weds 10% discount on 50 tickets, 15% on 100
Lewisham Public Baths Ladywell	2 1st & 2nd	1st & 2nd class 1d	every day from 6am to pm	-	90 x 70	-	-	-	school clubs to be established in connection with Board Schools and prizes be offered

1	2	3	4	5	6	7	8	9	10
Poplar, East India Dock Road	2 1st & 2nd		Sats 9 to 11am	-	1st 46 x 26 2nd 46 x 26				2 school clubs numbering 520 boys and 400 girls. Mostly Board School children attend these.
Rotherhithe Public Baths, Deptford Lower Road	2 1st & 2nd	2nd class bath 1d each	Tues Weds Thurs noon-2pm		1st 90 x 30 2nd 86 x 30				
St Giles in the Fields, Endell Street	2 1st & 2nd	1st class 2nd class 1d	Tues Weds Thurs Fri 9-11am	100	1st 36 x 24 2nd40 x 24	1 towel			women teachers must attend when bath used by girls
St Marylebone Public Baths	4 1st 2nd, 3rd, 4th	1st class 8d 200 tickets £4-15-0 2nd class 4d each, 200 tickets £2-10-0 3rd Class 2d each	-	-	1st 24 x25 2nd21 x 67 3rd 21 x67 4th 72 x26	-		commissioners have engaged swimming master who is prepared to teach large numbers of children at reduced prices	further facilities unavailable other than those stated
St Pancras, King Street	2 1st & 2nd	1st & 2nd 1d each	Boys, Mon - Fri 7:30-8:30pm Girls, Sats 10:30-11:30	50 50	1st 56 x22 2nd 56 x 22	1 towel			
Wandsworth High Road, Balham 12 The Exchange	2 1st & 2nd class	2½d each provided a sufficient number come at one time	Weds Sats 6-10am		1st 100 x 35 2nd 75 x 25		the proprietors would, to encourage swimming, return 5% of amount paid for admission, to be expended in prizes for annual competition by the children. If the number of children from each school who wish to bathe is given a price for the whole of the season for each school (irrespective) of numbers would be quoted.		
Westminster Public Bath	1	1d each child	Any day 12 Noon -1pm & 4-6pm. Other times by special arrangement. Specified hours could be arranged for the accommodation of girls	80	40 x 30	1 towel	The Bath attendant would give advice at all times		

Sub-Appendix C
(see page 54 of the main text)
Summary of Replies to questions addressed to the Official Correspondent of the Board

The following are examples only (Selected at random by the author and basically quoted verbatim)

	Baths	Charge	Swimming Club	Remarks
Finsbury Division Holloway Rd				
"Forster"	Private	1d	Yes	Boys instructed by
Blundell St	Baths	1d	Yes	members of Torpedo SC
Hackney Division				
Wilmot St	Working lads Instruction Private Bath Victoria Park Lakes	3d Towel found	No	Some of the boys use the Victoria Park Lakes
Olga St	People's Palace Private Baths	15 tickets for 1/-	No	The boys freely use Victoria Park Lakes.

If the Board could induce the LCC to make use of the lakes in Victoria Park more convenient and available for such children and to set apart a particular time for girls and could arrange with the authority of the People's Palace for the issue of tickets at reduced prices.

General Suggestions from Hackney
The Board should produce a list of Public Baths so that each school could use whatever accommodation is within reach.

1. It should further arrange with the authority
    (a) That a low fee should be charged
    (b) the bath should be reserved for the children at a certain convenient hour being particularly important for girls' schools. Many baths have no time set apart for women bathers.
    (c) the water be lowered at these times which is not difficult (as in Poplar) school times were reserved when water was let in or when schools had use one after another.
2. an attendant be provided or a swimming instructor to assist in starting clubs---- mainly necessary in girls' schools.
3. certificates and prizes given for competition.
4. The Board should make it understood that interest in such matters considered as adding to teachers value especially in promotion or appointment as headteachers. It should also be part of the special direction of managers.
5. suggest duties of managers to promote such clubs. Swimming might also be made part of the regular Pupil Teachers and Training College courses.

East Lambeth

There is an association called the "South London Schools Swimming Club" chiefly supported and managed by teachers and managers, in connection with which some, though not all, of the classes are carried on. Swimming classes are mainly around Peckham.

The association aims at securing bathing tickets for school children at specially reduced rates and using the funds for further reductions in the case of girls, providing teachers and awarding prizes.

The South-East London Swimming Club had presented a Silver Shield for competition by boys attending Board Schools and had promised a shield for competition by girls attending Board Schools.

There are no public baths in this division (i.e. baths provided by the local authority) in this division, but tickets, for children are issued at reduced prices by the proprietors of the Victoria Private Swimming Baths, St Martin's Road, Peckham. Most of the schools make use of those baths. The swimming class of one Board School, however, goes for practice to the Public Baths at Lewisham

A swimming class was formed in 1887 for the Bermondsey Schools by William Hunt, a local school Manager and Bath Commissioner, discontinued in 1888 on account of the illness of Mr Hunt and renewed in 1889. Tickets are sold to Head Teachers at 8/4 (100d) per 100. An entrance fee of 1d is charged, which goes towards supplying both dress and prizes. Tickets are sold to children at 1d. Practice Tuesdays, Wednesdays, Thursdays and Fridays 6 to 8am; 12:15 to 1:30pm; 4:30 to 6 pm.

Tuition

Exclusive use of the Bath, Thursdays 4:30 to 6pm. A teacher was to be in charge of each school. Special tickets for private warm baths on Thursdays 4:30 to 6pm.

In 1887 3,500 tickets were sold. 350 boys joined the class, seventy received certificates for ability to swim. In 1889 3,150 tickets sold. 418 boys and sixty girls joined the class. Fifty boys and five girls received certificates. Six silver medals were given as prizes. Forty boys joined the class from the Board's Evening classes and paid for 400 tickets at 3d. each. The boys' instructor was paid £3. Mrs Lane, formerly a teacher, in a Board School gave gratuitous instruction to the girls.

The total cost was £31-6-11, of which, only £11-8-1 had to be provided by friends in the locality.

The teachers assisted with great cordiality and attended and helped in teaching swimming. The Commissioners of Baths desire to encourage the classes.

There are excellent Public Baths in Rotherhithe but no arrangement was made for formation of swimming classes at the schools in the parish.

In West Southwark a special demand for swimming accommodation has come up from Orange Street and Pocock Street schools but there were no baths in that part of the division though the vestry of St George the Martyr adapted the Baths and Washhouses Acts some years ago.

Tower Hamlets

Baker Street	No swimming club. The People's Palace and the St Georges
Dempsey Street	Swimming Baths were suitable for these schools and would
Rutland Street	meet all the requirements of the neighbourhood.

Ben Jonson Single Street South Grove	No swimming club. The People's Palace and Victoria Park Lakes were the only places in neighbourhood where school children can bathe.
Berner Street Betts Street Lower Chapman Street	Yes. Swimming club. Public Baths in St Georges in the East including a large swimming bath and special facilities were provided for elementary school children to use these baths at reduced prices.
Browhouse Lane	Yes swimming club. A girls' club was formed during the summer months and meets at St George's Baths. The girls were taught by a professional instructor. Only a small fee was charged.
Buck's Row Darby Street Settles Street	No swimming club. In this neighbourhood exclusive access was provided and arrangements might easily have been made whereby swimming club for school children could be established.
Essex Street Portman Place	No swimming club. Only bathing accommodation is Victoria Park Lakes and the People's Palace Baths where a very small fee was charged.
Alton Street Farrance Street Morris Road	Yes, swimming club. Only Public Swimming Baths near this group of schools were the Poplar Swimming Baths, East India Dock Road. Classes meet and found May to September and prepaid fee of 1/6 per child. Prizes offered for competition and race meetings held at the baths. The classes were in connection with the Poplar Schools Swimming Club. At Farrance Street, 30 boys and 12 girls attend classes: at Alton Street 20 boys. No children authorised from Morris Road – the reason given was that they were too poor to pay the fee although it only amounted to about 1d a week. The managers suggested the fee should be collected from the children during the winter.
High Street Bromley Marner Street	No Swimming Club. No local efforts made to form Swimming Club although ample bathing bathing accommodation in neighbourhood.
Broad-street Collingwood Street "Highway"	Charge 1d. Yes Swimming Club. Swimming bath in Betts Street. St George's-in-the-East Bath open to school boys on Tuesdays from 7am to 9am and 12 noon to 2pm and on Saturdays from 6 to 9am on payments of 1d and to school girls on Tuesday from 4:30 to 6 pm on payment of 1d. The St George's-in-the-East Schools Swimming Club admits scholars from Board Schools in St George's-in-the-East, Wapping, Shadwell and Ratcliff. The club's annual subscription is 3d each

70

and certificates were awarded to those who learned to swim. It was hoped that a challenge shield would be offered for competition next year. Last season the girls were taught by 2 instructors. The instruction of the boys was left to voluntary help of Managers and teachers of the various schools. There was a great want of bathing accommodation in Ratcliff, the nearest bath being at least 20 minutes away.

Dalgleish St	Yes, swimming club East India Dock Road. ~~Poplar Public Baths~~ in Parish of Limehouse
Gill Street	No swimming club.
Northey Street	Yes, Swimming club, Boys 24.
Chicksand Street	No swimming club. For some years past, tickets for
Hanbury Street	admission to the Whitechapel Public Swimming baths have
Old Castle Street	been supplied to the boys attending the St Judes National Schools at a considerably reduced rate; prizes offered for competition by some of the Managers and much interest shown by boys. A swimming club is at Devenant School. The club meets at Gaulston Street baths. Admission 1d each.
Bromley Hall Road	Yes, swimming club. Boys
Brunswick Road	There is East India Dock Road, a large and highly popular
Byran and Bright Street	Public Baths successful club known as the Poplar Schools
Oban Street	Swimming Club which has now been established 9 years. Last
Orchard House Place	year the number of members was 519. Each boy paid 1/6 for the
Ricardo Street	season which entitled him to all the privileges of membership
St Leonard's Road	including use of the 1st class swimming bath at Poplar Baths
Upper North Street	for 18 successive Saturday mornings from 9 until 11 o'clock
Woolmore Street	and also 1 clean towel. The water was provided pure and tepid on every occasion. In addition every boy had also the chance of winning some of the valuable prizes given at the close of each season. These prizes usually amount in value to about £35 each year.

Girls

A Swimming club for girls was formed in May last year. 403 members joined during the summer. Subscriptions 1/6 for the season and similar advantages for boys. The girls also met for practice every Saturday am for 19/20 weeks through the summer in the 2nd class swimming bath of Poplar Baths and prizes distributed at end of season. These clubs are open to infinite expansion, open to any boy or girl paying subscriptions and have inclusive children from almost every Board School within a radius of 1½ miles from Poplar Baths. The School Board for London could render very important help by giving official instructions to the various head teachers of their schools to encourage children to join these clubs and also by offering suitable prizes to be competed for at the close of each season.

Atley Road Fairfield Road Smeed Road	No swimming club. The bathing accommodation in this district is lakes in Victoria Park, the People's Palace Baths and the Poplar Baths. A bath is about to be built in the Roman Road.
Cayley Street St John's Limehouse Trafalgar Square	No Swimming club. The People's Palace Baths is in the immediate neighbourhood of the schools and meets all requirements.
Knapp Road St Paul's Road Thomas Street	No Swimming club. Some of the children from this group of schools attend the People's Palace Baths. Teachers are in charge upon payment of a small fee. Others attend the Reverend R T Plummer's Bath or the Poplar Baths.

72

Sub-Appendix D
Table giving particulars of the provision made for Public Baths in London

School Board Division	Provision under Baths and Washhouses Act	Provision by Private Enterprise
City of London	-	-
Chelsea	Lancaster Road 3	171 King's Road 2 Melmouth Place, Walham Green 2 Black's Road 1
Finsbury	Endell Street 2	Fonthill Road 2 Junction Road 1 166 Holloway Road 2 Liverpool Road 1 Pentonville Road 2 St John's Street 1 Finsbury Polytechnic 1
Greenwich	London Street 2 Dartmouth Road, Forest Hill 2 Ladywell Road 2	
Hackney		Bethnal Green Road 2 Albion Baths, Albion Square 1 Metropolitan Baths, 89 (?) Shepherdess Walk 2 Wenlock Road 1
East Lambeth		St Martin's-Road, Peckham 2 Addington Square, Camberwell 1
West Lambeth	Latchmere Road 2	York Road 1 Westminster,Bridge Road 2 Kennington Oval, (Crown Baths) 2 Polytechnic, Ferndale Road 1 High-road, Balham 2 Putney Bridge Road 1
Marylebone	Finchley New Road 3 Queen's Road Bayswater 4	

181 Marylebone Road 4
King-street, Camden Town 2
Whitfield Court Tottenham Court
Road 2

Southwark	39 Spa Road 2	
	Deptford Lower Road 2	
Tower Hamlets	Betts-street 1	People's Palace 1
	East India Dock Road 2	305 East India Dock Road 1
	Gaulston Street 2	Working Lads Institute 1
Westminster	Davies Street 1	
	Buckingham Palace Road 2	
	16 Marshall Street 1	

Totals

School Board Divisions	11
Parliamentary Divisions	58
Population Census 1881	3,771,289
Swimming Baths provided under the Baths and Washhouses Acts	19 Establishments with 41 Baths
Swimming Baths provided by Private Enterprise	25 Establishments with 36 Baths

---

Notes

1. School Board for London, *Report of the Physical Education Sub-Committee on Bathing Accommodation and Swimming Classes (Public Elementary Schools) with Appendices*, 1-41, Charles Straker & Sons, printers to the Board, Bishopsgate Avenue, London EC, May 1890.
2. School Management Sub-Committee, Special Subjects Sub-Committee, School Board for London, *Swimming Return Shewing (A) Results of Instruction in Swimming during the year ended Lady-Day 1903 (B) Existing and Projected Swimming Baths © Timetables of Swimming Baths for 1903 Season*, 1-19, Southwood Smith & Co Ltd., Printers to the Board, 1903.
3. PP XXV, 1886: PP XXIX + XXX, 1887: PP XXXV-XXXVII, 1888; *Reports of the Royal Commission to enquire into the working of the Elementary Education Acts*, 1886-1888.
4. May, Jonathan, *Madame Bergman-Osterberg, Pioneer of Physical Education and Games for Girls and Women*, 13, Published for The University of London Institute of Education, by George G. Harrap &Co Ltd., London, 1969.
5. School Board for London, Appendix A, 'Report submitted to the Board by the Works Committee on the 26 June 1872', 13, in op. cit., *Report of the Physical Education Sub-Committee on Bathing Accommodation & Swimming Classes*, May 1890.

APPENDIX III
CHARLIE WARNER MEDALLISTS AT THE DORKING
BRITISH (POWELL-CORDEROY) SCHOOL 1897-1938 (SURREY)
Source SHC C/ES/115/2/4/44

1897	Wesley Turner	1919	Cyril Aldred
1898	Percy Jeal	1920	Ernest Gegg
1899	Thomas Warner	1921	Alfred Lynch
1900	Norman Spratling	1922	Basil Conway
1901	Horace Weeks	1923	Leonard Dobson
1902	Harry Borer	1924	Eric Smith
1903	Harold Jeal	1925	Robert James
1904	Norman Cousin	1926	Albert Davidson
1905	Edward Letts	1927	Dan James
1906	Fred Scragg	1928	Percy Aldred
1907	George Webb	1929	Eric Overton
	Leslie Fuller	1930	James Chapman
1908	Clifford Smith	1931	Ronald Arlett
1909	William Butler	1932	John Orr
1910	James Webb	1933	John Orr
1911	Herbert Vine	1934	Stanley Cutler
	Leonard Kellow	1935	Frank Cutler
	(saved boy's life)	1936	Frank Cutler
1912	George Wilkins	1937	Edmund Miller
1913	Frank Walker	1938	Peter Rapley
1914	Edward Moore		
1915	Robert Martin	Dorking Urban Swimming Bath
1916	Arthur Butler	was subsequently closed.
1917	Walter Dennis		
1918	Tom Turner		

APPENDIX IV
DORKING BRITISH SCHOOLS
PROGRAMME FOR THE 7TH ANNUAL SWIMMING SPORTS
21 SEPTEMBER 1904 (SURREY)
Source: SHC C/ES/115/2/1/1

Programme.

~~~EVENTS.~~~

I. BEGINNERS' WIDTH (Boys). Two Prizes.

1 E. Harrison   3 W. Butler
2 F. Elms

II. BEGINNERS' WIDTH (Girls). Two Prizes.

1 L. Brett   4 G. Bailey
2 E. Geall   5 L. Songhurst
3 D. Cousin

Width for Girl — L. Luurst 1st Griffith i

III. ONE LENGTH (Boys). Three Prizes.

1st HEAT.
1 J. Griffiths .... scratch
2 J. Stokes .... 1 sec.
3 F. Scragg .... 1 sec.
4 C. Webb .... 1 sec.
5 W. Marshall .... 2 secs.

2nd HEAT.
1 E. Tanner .... scratch
2 R. Butler .... 2 secs.
3 E. Letts .... 2 secs.
4 H. Humby .... 7 secs.

3rd HEAT.
1 A. Woods .... scratch
2 H. Steer .... 2 secs.
3 G. Webb .... 2 secs.
4 W. Butler .... 7 secs.

1st in each heat and fastest loser to swim in final.

G. Webb 1.
R. Butler 2.
J. Griffiths 3.

IV. ONE LENGTH HANDICAP (Girls). One Prize.

1 Jessie Griffiths .... scratch
2 Hilda Warner .... 5 secs.

Swimming Two Lengths under water by B. W. Turner. *Successful.*

V. "C.W." MEDAL

TWO LENGTHS SCRATCH. The Medal is presented annually by MISS CORDEROY in memory of the late CHARLIE WARNER, son of Mr. T. C. WARNER. Competitors must be scholars of the Dorking British School of at least 12 months' standing. The competitor obtaining the highest number of marks for *Running Dive, Plunge, and Swimming Two Lengths of the Bath* scores the Medal. Two Prizes.

1 E. Tanner   4 R. Butler
2 J. Stokes   5 W. Jeal
3 J. Griffiths   6 A. N. Cousin

Winner of Medal

Previous Winners:
1897. Wesley Turner
1898. Percy Jeal
1899. Thomas Warner
1900. Norman Sparling
1901. Horace Weeks
1902. Harry Borer
1903. H. Jeal

Swimming without Tiring—T. Warner.

VI. PLUNGING (including "C.W." Medal). Three Prizes.

1 W. Marshall   7 A. N. Cousin
2 J. Stokes   8 E. Harrison
3 E. Tanner   9 A. Woods
4 W. Jeal   10 R. Butler
5 J. Griffiths   11 H. Steer
6 E. Letts

VII. OLD BOYS' HANDICAP—TWO LENGTHS. Three Prizes.

1st HEAT.
1 B. W. Turner .... scratch
2 P. Jeal .... 2 secs.
3 Herbert Stokes .... 6 secs.

2nd HEAT.
1 W. P. Jeal .... 1 sec.
2 E. Jacocks .... 5 secs.
3 H. Jeal .... 5 secs.

3rd HEAT.
1 J. Caven .... 2 secs.
2 Hy. Stokes .... 5 secs.
3 E. Croucher .... 7 secs.

3—1st in each heat and fastest loser to swim in final.

1st W. Turner 1st
1 Jacock 2nd
W. P. Jeal

VIII. THREE LENGTHS HANDICAP. Three Prizes.

1st HEAT.
1 W. Rumbold .... scratch
2 J. Griffiths .... 8 secs.
3 R. Butler .... 10 secs.

2nd HEAT.
1 N. Cousin .... 4 secs.
2 J. Stokes .... 9 secs.
3 E. Tanner .... 10 secs.

1. A. Cousin
2. W. Rumbold
3. J. Stokes

IX. OLD BOYS—FINAL.

APPENDIX V
GIRLS' CHAMPIONSHIP MEDALLISTS
AT THE DORKING BRITISH (POWELL-CORDEROY) SCHOOL
1908-1938

Source: SHC C/ES/115/2/4/44 Log Book 1889-1919 page 219

Year	Medallist	Year	Medallist
1908	Grace Bailey	1924	Gwen Conway
1909	Lucy Truin	1925	Frances Gater
1910	Madge Williams	1926	Margaret Gater
1911	Gladys Plummer	1927	Joan Rogerson
1912	Florence Edwards	1928	May Clarke
1913	May Carpenter	1929	Gladys Dennis
1914	Mollie Pett	1930	Gladys Dennis
1915	Nellie Pank	1931	Joan Smith
1916	Norah Andrews	1932	Ivy Stokes
1917	Eileen Gore	1933	Joan Dennis
1918	—	1934	Ivy Stokes (saved girl's life)
1919	Ivy Rich	1935	Irene Godwin
1920	Mabel Jackson	1936	Irene Godwin
1921	Constance Conway	1937	Barbara Stonestreet
1922	—	1938	Barbara Stonestreet
1923	Rita Dobson		

Dorking UDC Baths closed.

APPENDIX VI
BATHING PLACES IN SURREY IN 1912
Source: Sachs, Frank, The Complete Swimmer, 259

Brockham	River Mole
Dorking	Public Baths, Station Road River Mole at Castle Mill
Epsom	Private Bath, Royal Medical College
Earlswood	Public Bath, Earlswood; Lake, Earlswood Common
Farnham	Public Bath, South Street, Open Air
Guildford	Public Bath, Guildford
Godalming	Private Bath, Charterhouse School, River Wey
Horley	River Mole at Six Bells
Leatherhead	Public Bath, Bridge Street, River Mole
Redhill	Private Bath, Royal Asylum of St Anne's Society School Private Bath, Philanthropic Society's Farm School, Open Air
Reigate	Public Bath, Castle Fields Road Private Bath, St David's School, Open Air
Sutton	Public Bath, Throwley Road
Shere	Public Bath, Church Field, Open Air
Walton	Public Bath, Thames. Mixed Bathing
Weybridge	River Thames, Ladies, Wednesdays 10 till 1, 2 till 4
Woking	River Wey

APPENDIX VII
THE ORIGINS OF SWIMMING IN GUILDFORD'S ELEMENTARY SCHOOLS (SURREY)

The Surrey Times[1] noted that the Guildford Swimming Club and Life Saving Society (local branch) held a swimming entertainment at the Guildford Baths on Wednesday 7 September 1898. Alderman A Allen presided in the absence of the mayor. He noted that there was something missing in the art of swimming in Guildford schools. He was sure that everyone regretted the time had not arrived when swimming was part of the educational system. He had wondered that if special prizes were offered to the children of the schools, it would be an inducement to teachers to take up the art of swimming. He suggested that the schools should find their two or three best swimmers and a final competition could be arranged in the annual sports of the club. If that were possible then he, Alderman Alder, would be prepared to donate a challenge cup to be competed for by schools in the Guildford area. Were that to be arranged he would also be glad to arrange to give a prize to the winner.

A further report[2] on the subject did not appear until May 1900 under the heading School Children and Swimming. A meeting was convened at the headquarters of Guildford Swimming Club, Quarry Hill on Monday 14 May 1900. The purpose was to promote the art of swimming among the elementary schools and to draw up the rules of the competition for the Elementary Schools Challenge Cup donated by Arthur Allen. Among those who attended were: Mr Allen, WL Jones, A Leroy, SW Bird, WR Harris of the Guildford Swimming Club and representatives from the following schools: Abbot's, Charlotteville, Holy Trinity, Saint Nicolas, Stoke and Stoughton.

The meeting decided to ask the managers of the various schools to add swimming to their curriculum and to approach the corporation to increase the facilities for boys to attend the baths at convenient times for practice during school hours.

At a further entertainment[3] on Wednesday 30 May 1900, the Mayor noted that a memorial had been received from the ratepayers of the town that sought to establish swimming for school boys and girls at the baths. The Town Council was anxious to support the memorial but they had to act within the law since the baths were provided by the ratepayers. However, they could not legally set aside the bath for the use of one class of persons to the exclusion of others. A council meeting on Friday would try to resolve the difficulties involved.

Notes
1. *The Surrey Times*, 10 September 1898, 6.
2. ibid., 19 May 1900, 5.
3. ibid., 2 June 1900, 6.

APPENDIX VIII
SWIMMING IN SUTTON'S ELEMENTARY SCHOOLS
(SURREY)

The Sutton Advertiser[1] reported the gathering of a large number of children at the Sutton Baths on the finals of the inter-school swimming competitions inaugurated in 1911 by the School Sports Association under the patronage of the County Education Committee and the aegis of the local school managers.

The first event was an inter-school team race for girls, the winning team to hold the shield presented by Councillor Russell Davis who also gave medals to the winning team. Crown Road, New Town and Holy Trinity Wallington were entered with New Town finishing first, Crown Road second and Wallington third.

A similar race was next for boys. Six teams were entered: Beddington, Benhilton, Crown Road, New Town, Wallington and West Street. The winning team was Wallington with New Town second and Benhilton third. Wallington received a shield presented by Messrs Pile and medals were again given by Councillor Davis.

Next, was a fifty yards scratch inter-school championship race for girls with one entrant from each school. New Town were the winners with Crown Road two feet behind with Benhilton and Wallington trailing.

In the similar boys' race Beddington did not compete. New Town won with Crown Road coming in second.

The Rector presented the prizes to:

New Town Girls: Amy Price,Lucy McGowan, Mabel Leaver and May Goldsmith.
Wallington Boys: Bertram Darrant, Ernest Baker, Harold Kelly and George Snape.
Girls' Championship: 1. (prize by Mrs R H Knight) May Goldsmith (New Town)
                       2. (prize by Mr R Ashton) Lily Cutts (Crown Road)
Boys' Championship: 1. (Prize by Mr R W Wootten) E Garner (New Town)
                       2. (prize presented by the Dolphin S Club) Cecil Jaggs (Benhilton).

The Rector presented certificates issued by the Sutton Urban District Council and similar swimming certificates presented by the SCC. After hearty thanks all round the Rector said that this had not been an entertainment but rather part of the course of education of the children. It had been arranged at very short notice and organised very well. He was surprised at the proficiency of the scholars, which reflected well on the the teaching force from Captain Mignon down to the junior teachers.

It was subsequently reported[2] that Mr White, headmaster of the Benhilton Schools, had criticised that the Boys' championship had been decided by breast stroke since Jaggs was best at side stroke and thus lost the chance to win the championship. On Friday, the previous Friday (29 September) he had issued an invitation to each of the competing schools to send a representative to the baths on the following Monday to contest two lengths on a "go as you please" basis. Only J Salter of West Street, who had finished third in the original race, turned up. Jaggs won in the excellent time of forty-nine seconds, which was one and three-fifths seconds faster than the winner's time in the original race. He thus established *the right* (*author's italics*) to be deemed the champion swimmer of the local schools!

Subsequently, Mr White presented the winner with four bound volumes and to J Salter, the other lad, he presented one volume and commended his sportsmanship in turning up. Mr GC Seeviour, headmaster of West Street, was present along with several other assistant masters.

The second annual swimming sports, under the auspices of the Sutton and District Elementary Day Schools' Sports Association, were held on Wednesday 31 July 1912.[3] The programme was much longer than in the inaugural year.

School Team Championship for Girls for the Russell Davis Challenge Shield over twenty-five yards breast stroke
1.   Newtown Sutton, Amy Price, Connie Walpole, Jessie Winters and Muriel Hare
2.   Crown Road Sutton, Rose Dixon, Ivy Money, Alice Wellman and May Card

School Team Championship for Boys for the "Herald" Challenge Shield also over twenty-five yards breast stroke
1.   Newtown, S Adams,G Levett, H Garner and A Cocking
2.   Benhilton, H Hill, E Newby, E Halse and C Jaggs
3.   Crown Road, F Oxford, J Oxford, G Page and R Swann
4.   West Street, F Underwood, F Stevens, J Cook and V Hancock

School Championsip fifty yards Girls
1.   Ivy Money (Crown Road)
2.   Connie Walpole

School Championship fifty yards Boys
1.   W Jaggs (Benhilton)
2.   S Adams (Newtown)

Breast Stroke Championship over fifty yards for Girls
1.   Rose Dixon (Crown Road)

Breast Stroke Championship over fifty yards for Boys
1.   C Jaggs (Benhilton)
2.   H Garner (Newtown)
3.   G Prentice (Camden Road, Carshalton)

Diving:
Girls   Daisy Prior, (Newtown)

Boys
1.   W Jaggs (Benhilton 29? points)
2.   W Waylan (Beddington, 23 points)
3.   G Levett (Newtown 21 points)

82

Junior Championship – Girls under 13, twenty-five yards breaststroke
Nora McGowan (Newtown)
Junior Championship – Boys under 13, twenty-five yards breaststroke
1.   A Cocking (Newtown)
2.   J Oxford (Crown-road)
3.   V Mantell (West-street)

Old Scholars – Girls under 17, fifty yards
Heat I
1.   M Goldsmith (Newtown)
2.   M Atkins (Crown Road)

Heat II
1.   M Leaver (Newtown)
2.   W Morris (Newtown)

Final
1.   M Goldsmith (Newtown)
2.   M Leaver (Newtown)
3.   W Morris (Newtown)
4.   M Atkins (Crown Road)

Old Scholars – Boys under 17, fifty yards
Heat I
1.   S Levett (Newtown)
2.   H Horsley (Camden Road)
3.   J Salter (West-street)
Heat II
1.   S Triggs (Newtown)
2.   G Simmonds (Crown Road)
3.   G Graves (Camden Road)
Final
1.   S Levett (Newtown)
2.   J Salter (West Street)
3.   H Horsley (Camden Road)

Putt(?) race twenty-five yards
1.   E Newby (Benhilton)
2.   A Winter (Bedlington)

Walking The Pole
1.   V Hancock (West Street)
2.   G Barnett (Beddington)

Notes
1.   *The (Sutton) Advertiser*, 29 September 1911, 6.
2.   ibid., 6 October 1911, 3.
3.   ibid., 2 August 1912, 5.

APPENDIX IX
SWIMMING AT THE GODALMING NATIONAL BOYS' SCHOOL AND THE EGHAM HYTHE BOYS' AND GIRLS' SCHOOLS (SURREY)

Selected and edited entries at the Godalming National Boys' School
Log Book opened 1 May 1863

1 February 1907, page 308.
Major Norman called on Tuesday regarding the formation of a swimming class during the summer months

3 June 1907, page 314.
Have arranged to start a swimming class with the upper class in place of physical exercises in the playground. The weather is much too cold today to commence.

14 June 1907, page 315.
The first class have commenced their swimming lessons making two this week in place of drill in the playground.

18 July 1907, page 317.
Sergeant Mills called in the afternoon and went up to see the swimming. I (William Barnfield) found 15 boys who could swim nearly all of whom had learnt since the commencement of the class.

29 July 1907, page 317.
Major Norman came to see the swimming class. He found the second class (under Mr Taylor) being examined and spoke highly of their work.

26 September 1907, page 319.
The boys went up for the last swimming lesson of the season, the Bathing Station being closed at the end of the week. I find 21 boys have learnt to swim.

5 June 1908, page 332.
The first swimming lesson of the season.

21 January 1910, page 362.
Received 12 swimming certificates from the SEC

26 September 1910, page 375.

The swimming class went up for the last lesson this season. 16 boys were tested and qualified for certificates for distances varying from 20 to 30 yards.

6 June 1912, page 405.

Commenced swimming lessons for the season sending up Standard V and upwards.

Log Book closed 29 May 1914

Log Book opened 9 June 1914

20 May 1919, page 75.

Swimming classes recommenced at the Charterhouse Open Air Bathing Station (Tuesday and Friday afternoons 3:15pm to 4pm)

17 September 1920, page 92.

Swimming lessons continued though the weather has not been favourable.

22 September 1922, page 117.

Miss Le Couteur visited regarding arrangements for a Schools' Swimming Competition for the Leon Shield.

26 September 1922, page 117.

The swimming Competition was held at the Swimming Baths at Guildford last evening, our boys winning the trophy. The contest included a team race and a diving competition.

26 April 1923, page 125. A L Leon visited-donor of the swimming trophy.

26 September 1924, page 145.

The swimming season finished this afternoon. The season has been very wet, cold and generally unfavourable for outdoor swimming.

3 October 1944, page 145.

Notice received that the Inter-School Swimming Competition for the Leon Trophy will take place at the Guildford Baths on Wednesday 8th at 6pm.

9 October 1924, page 145.

The swimming team went to the Guildford Swimming Baths for the "Leon" contest last evening and did very well gaining the highest number of marks, but there is to be added a certain number of points for number of new swimmers.

28 October 1924, page 146.

Miss Le Couteur visited during the afternoon bringing the Leon Trophy which she presented to the team.

28 September 1925, page 157.

Mr Walker and 5 boys, J Colpus, J Mullins, E Caesar, R Tubbs and N Piercey went to Dorking to compete in the Swimming Competition for the Leon Trophy, of which we are the holders.

24 September 1926, page 170.
Elementary Schools (Open Air Swimming Baths) competition held at Reigate.

27 September 1926, page 171.
The boys finished 3rd in the competition.

7 October 1927, page 183.
I have taken 7 boys to Guildford this afternoon for the Leon Trophy and in accordance with the instructions their attendances have been reckoned. The team were second. Other results were:

       8 gained County Certificates
       9 qualified for endorsement
       11 swam 8-25 yards

10 October 1928, page 197.
       15 qualified for the County Certificates of 50 yards
       9 qualified for further endorsement
       6 can swim up to 20 yards

30 September 1929, page 207.
       14 County Certificates
       16 endorsements (100-1800 yards)
       6 less than 25 yards

12 October 1931, page 229.
Annual Elementary Schools Competition at Guildford held at Guildford Swimming Baths on the 7th. Team finished 2nd, Leatherhead Central 1st.

12 May 1932, page 236.
Received notice that the Bathing Place would not be available for schools during afternoons.

27 September 1932, page 240.
Team tied with Leatherhead Central for the Leon Trophy which we hold for 1st half of year.

20 June 1933, page 248.
Miss Le Couteur called regarding swimming. I told her I had agreed to the change under protest.

27 February 1934, page 255.
Following a meeting of headteachers with Alderman PC Fletcher, our swimming lessons have been fixed for Tuesday 3:30-4pm and Friday 3:30-4pm.

27 September 1934, page 260.
In the afternoon, six boys went to take part in the Elementary schools County Swimming Competition.

27 September 1935, page 269.
Swimming Competition at Guildford Baths. Mr Walker took 6 boys to compete.

Egham Hythe Boys School
Log Book opened 15 March 1886

13 June 1907, page 284.
Major Norman visited regarding the Swimming Club.

15 July 1907, page 287.
Received notice that the boys might commence their swimming lessons this week – 10 swimmers and 10 non-swimmers at each lesson on Monday and Friday 3:45 to 5pm.

28 February 1908, page 298.
Wrote to Major Norman regarding swimming as he wanted 20 boys to be guaranteed regular lessons.

5 May 1908, page 304.
Major Norman wrote about swimming: "The same number and under the same conditions as last season-but-once a week as long as bathing season lasts."

21 May 1908, page 304.
Swimming lessons commenced today 40 boys to go per week 20 each on Monday and Thursdays at 3:30.

24 July 1908, page 312.
Silver Challenge Cup won in open juvenile races at Chertsey yesterday; C and E Oades, A Hawkins and VF Gardner.

18 September 1908, page 314.
Copy of numbers of swimming class sent to the Instructor of Physical Drill
>   40 in the 2 classes sent
>   9 cannot swim yet
>   9 can swim a few yards
>   10 can swim 30 yards
>   9 can swim over a 100 yards
>   3 left

26 July 1909, page 332.
George Tyler drowned whilst trying to rescue Leslie Case who also drowned. This happened after the boys had their swimming lesson and had entered the water a second time on their way home. Mr Baldwin dived for the lads but failed to locate them.

10 November 1909, page 336.
A silver medal given by the proprietors of the Middlesex Chronicle was presented to the father of George Tyler for his heroism in trying to save the life of Leslie Case but was unfortunately drowned on the attempt.

Egham School Girls
Log Book Opened 15 March 1886

9 January 1911, page 275.
7 girls have obtained Certificates for proficiency in swimming.

20 May 1912, page 283.
This afternoon 15 girls had instruction in swimming, being the first lesson of the session.

3 June 1912, page 283.
First class will exchange History and Grammar lessons on Mondays owing to some girls attending swimming lessons.

14 May 1914, page 295.
Commenced lessons in swimming this afternoon.

APPENDIX X
SUMMARY OF RESULTS OF INSTRUCTION IN SWIMMING GIVEN AT BATHS UNDER THE CONTROL OF METROPOLITAN BOROUGH COUNCILS DURING THE YEAR ENDED LADY DAY 1903

Source: School Board for London: School Management Sub-committee, Special Subjects Sub-committee Supplement to Swimming Return for the year ended Lady-Day 1903.

Key: B = Boys, G = Girls, M =Mixed, T = Totals.

	Schools swimming under Board's Scheme	No. of departments				No. of scholars in those schools eligible to receive instruction in departments				No. of scholars instructed				No.of scholars taught to swim			
		B	G	M	T	B	G	M	T	B	G	M	T	B	G	M	T
Battersea	16	15	6		21	3,788	1,492		5,280	2,196	322		2,518	592	72		664
Bermondsey	28	22	16	1	39	4,421	3,079	160	7,660	2,487	559	65	3,111	731	166	20	917
Bethnal Green	-	-	-	-	-	-	-	-	-	-	-	-	-	-	-	-	-
Camberwell	23	22	6		28	4,642	1,485		6,127	2,797	358		3,149	605	71		676
Chelsea	3	3	1		4	573	221		794	291	60		351	145	16		161
City Corp	-	-	-	-	-	-	-	-	-	-	-	-	-	-	-	-	-
Deptford	16	13	4	2	19	2,525	775	329	3,629	1,522	179	162	1,863	400	57	50	507
Finsbury	-	-	-	-	-	-	-	-	-	-	-	-	-	-	-	-	-
Fulham	16	15	9	2	26	2,949	2,181	618	5,748	1,713	370	309	2,392	593	162	119	874
Greenwich	6	4	2	1	7	644	408	206	1,258	371	71	79	521	118	36	35	189
Hackney	22	17	10	5	32	3,863	2,547	1,021	7,431	2,160	671	364	3,195	763	317	131	1,211
Hammersmith	-	-	-	-	-	-	-	-	-	-	-	-	-	-	-	-	-
Hampstead	1	1			1	203			203	48			48	24			24
Holborn	3	1	1	1	3	43	78	12	133	53	38	4	95	25	12		37
Islington	42	36	23	2	61	7,036	4,848	539	12,423	4,369	1594	349	6,312	1,331	589	88	2,008
Kennington	1	1			1	199			199	140			140	33			33
Lambeth	11	8	7		15	1,373	1,463		2,836	721	387		1,108	242	157		399
Lewisham	9	7	5	2	14	1,592	1,210	609	3,411	643	312	252	1,207	212	96	47	355
Paddington	4	2	1	2	5	515	188	645	1,348	249	53	100	402	88	23	41	152
Poplar	25	24	8	1	33	4,562	1,833	89	6,484	2,022	439	60	2,521	627	110	12	749
St Marylebone	3	2	1		3	372	94		466	168	68		236	67	3		7
St Pancras	15	13	10	1	24	2,424	2,483	469	5,376	1,287	773	137	2,197	416	287	64	767
Shoreditch	16	15	6	1	22	2,747	939	50	3,736	1,778	422	20	2,220	729	123	5	944
Southwark	27	26	12	1	39	4,931	2,118	7	7,056	2,686	620	16	3,322	738	201	5	944
Stepney	18	13	14	3	30	2,355	2,684	627	5,666	863	629	230	1,722	274	242	92	608
Stoke Newington	-	-	-	-	-	-	-	-	-	-	-	-	-	-	-	-	-
Wandsworth	7	6	6		12	1,308	1,176		2,484	1,007	396		1,403	310	154		464
Westminster	6	6	3	1	10	608	279	5	892	484	119	5	608	197	45		242
Woolwich	11	9	8	1	18	1,401	1,358	5	2,764	750	444	2	1,196	241	193	2	436

APPENDIX XI
SUMMARY OF SCHOOLS NOT TAKING SWIMMING UNDER THE BOARD'S SCHEME (LONDON)
Source: as Appendix X

Key: B = Boys, G = Girls, M =Mixed, T = Totals.

	No. of Schools Not Taking Swimming under Board's Scheme	No. of Departments				No. of scholars in these schools eligible to receive instruction in Swimming		
		B	G	M	T	B	G	T
Battersea	12	3	12	1	16	820	2,918	3,738
Bermondsey	9	1	9		10	219	1,616	1,835
Bethnal Green	15	2	13	2	17	325	2,297	2,622
Camberwell	29	8	25	2	35	2,076	5,667	7,743
Chelsea	3	2	2		4	362	374	736
City Corp	1			1	1	46	44	90
Deptford	10	4	9	2	15	803	1,750	2,553
Finsbury	10	7	10		17	1,268	1,562	2,830
Fulham	10	3	9		12	607	1,800	2,407
Greenwich	14	7	11	2	20	1,318	2,009	3,327
Hackney	15	2	10	7	19	420	1,815	2,235
Hammersmith	11	7	9	3	19	1,783	2,309	4,092
Hampstead	6	1	2	5	8	845	1,120	1,965
Holborn	5	5	5		10	563	608	1,171
Islington	17	4	16	1	21	1,197	3,490	4,687
Kennington	11	9	11		20	1,860	2,008	3,868
Lambeth	17	10	15	3	28	2,595	3,325	5,920
Lewisham	7	3	4	4	11	823	1,019	1,842
Paddington	4		2	2	4	277	686	963
Poplar	19	7	17	3	27	1,385	2,970	4,355
St Marylebone	6	5	7		12	749	1,088	1,837
St Pancras	10	6	7	2	15	1,509	1,168	2,677
Shoreditch	5		5		5		1,154	1,184
Southwark	14	2	12		14	331	2,104	2,435
Stepney	21	7	17	5	29	1,297	3,193	4,490
Stoke Newington	4	4	4		8	955	968	1,923
Wandsworth	20	9	11	10	30	2,694	2,998	5,692
Westminster	2				2		157	157
Woolwich	17	10	10	7	27	2,265	2,539	4,804

APPENDIX XII
SWIMMING 1907 (SURREY)

Source: Appendix MI dd. 2 January 1908 in 22nd Report of the SEC dd. 11 February 1908.

School	Numbers Taught To Swim		Numbers Exercised in Life-Saving Practice	General Remarks
Dorking				
Westcott	Boys	11	A few children had practised these exercises	The children of this school had a long way to go to the bath. The coldness of the season and an epidemic of whooping cough had tended to lessen the attendance. Still the boys attended on 24 occasions, the girls on 21. Suggested that 12 free tickets be given instead of 9.
	Girls	4		
National	Boys	12	8 (6 Certificates)	This school had done extremely well, due, perhaps, in some measure to the boys having been granted many more free tickets than those of other local schools, but, chiefly to the excellent instruction of Mr Jay, one of the school staff. This school took first prize in nearly every event of the Inter-School Swimming Sports.
	Girls	8	6 (1 Certificate)	
St Paul's	Boys	7	6 (5 Certificates)	A very keen swimming school. The somewhat late announcement as to the number of free tickets to be given upset the arrangements for the season. Suggested that 12 tickets be given in place of 9, and some "season" tickets and the scheme issued earlier in the year.
	Girls	6	7 (7 Certificates)	
British	Boys	9	18 have practised these exercises	Suggested that free tickets should be extended to Standard V. A good swimming school, and much interest taken.
	Girls	11		
Farnham				
East Street		10	12	A very good swimming and physical training school. Won the local Swimming Shield, and many events in the Inter-Schools Swimming Competition, due I consider to the keen interest taken by the Headmaster and Staff.
West Street		8	0	A good swimming school: will run East Street close another year.
St Polycarp's		5	6	An exceptionally good school for its size. Won open events in the Inter-School Competition. The swimming instruction of this school was given by Mr Bonelli, a local gentleman, who devoted a great deal of his time in advancing the swimming and physical training of St Polycarp's.
Bourne		7	0	A good school greatly handicapped by the distance of the swimming bath.

School		Boys/Girls	Num1	Num2	Comments
Hale			7	0	As above. There was a question of a swimming bath at Hale itself, and, if this was provided, the interest taken by the Headmaster and Staff would guarantee the school taking a high place as a swimming school.
Badshot Lea			7	0	A long way from the bath. Every encouragement given by the headmaster and staff.
Wrecclesham			6	0	A long way from the bath. An attempt was made to obtain use of a local stream, but failed. Under the circumstances this season's results were very creditable.
Sutton					
New Town	Boys		20	0	A first-rate school. The arrangements for the girls were not made till too late in the season, or more would have learned to swim. I hope to obtain from the Bath authorities a longer period for the use of the bath by elementary school children, and so enable other local schools, such as Benhilton to take part. Two of the mistresses took lessons and learnt to swim.
	Girls		11	0	
West Street			7	0	A good school. Two of the pupils took 1st and 2nd prize in a scholars' handicap.
Crown Rd	Boys		12	0	Good work done, but, as above, more facilities much desired. Very good work considering the short course shown by the girls. One mistress took swimming lessons.
	Girls		11	0	
Ham Common			18	0	Great interest shown in swimming, and excellent work done. The girls were overlooked in this year's scheme, which was all the more regrettable as the mistresses at this school had taken swimming very keenly.
Surbiton					
Tolworth	Boys		16	0	Great interest taken by the head teachers and staff and capital work done. This school was a long way from the bath. A larger number of tickets was desired and that they should be issued earlier in the season, and that certain swimming apparatus be provided.
	Girls		3	0	
St Mark's	Boys		17	2	Good work. Interest in swimming had for many years been shown in this school.
C of E, New Malden			15	0	Headmaster and Staff had taken up swimming keenly. Suggested that tickets be issued not later than 1st May.
Long Ditton	Boys		5	0	A long way from the bath. This prevented the girls of this school, availing themselves of the free tickets provided for them.
Christ Church Surbiton			16	0	A keen swimming school; a long way from the bath.
Thames Ditton			6	0	No free tickets were provided for this school. The Headmater had obtained permission to use the bathing place of the Trotting Club Association in the River Imber, and parties of 30 were taken down out of school hours. The Headmaster and four of his staff are keen swimmers. Suggested that a small grant be given to clear the river bed and to provide a rope to stretch across as a further safeguard.

Merton	Boys	50	0	A first rate swimming school. The interest taken in swimming was of long standing, and was fostered by the old boys of the school, several of whom had given valuable cups for competition.

Godalming

National		18	0	Bathing takes place in the Wey. The bad weather had naturally been against bathing in the open, still strong parties went to swim twice a week, one of the staff usually being in the bath with them. Much assistance was rendered by the care taken; those services deserved recognition.
Walton-on-Thames	Boys	16	0	Mr Clarke's floating bath at Walton was used. It is suggested that the classes be smaller, so that more individual instruction be given. As the agreement for the use of this bath included professional instruction, and the classes were larger than elsewhere, the results do not compare favourably with those of Sutton, New Town (Girls), for instance, where the instruction was given by the School Staff.
	Girls	3	0	
Oatlands	Boys	1	0	As above. An epidemic of measles interfered with the swimming arrangements, and bathing was altogether suspended for some weeks.
Horley, Lumley Rd	Boys	8	0	The school obtained the use of the private bathing place of the Horley Swimming Club. The cold summer affected the attendance. This school made a good beginning, and all were keen. Suggested that a few belts be provided to aid instruction.
Egham, Hythe	Boys	15	0	Arrangements for swimming were made late in the season, which was in consequence a short one.
Egham, Station Rd	Boys	6	0	As above
Holmbury St Mary's	Boys	6	0	Children of this school had free use of, and free instruction in, a swimming bath built by a local gentleman. During the last 7 years 61 boys and girls had been taught to swim. This season 6 boys and 5 girls were shown as having learnt, though in a competition there were 19 boys swam the length of the bath which was 60 feet long.
	Girls	6	0	

APPENDIX XIII
RESULTS OF THE 1909 SEASON[1] (SURREY)

Name of School		Numbers Attending	Numbers Taught To Swim	Numbers Gaining County Certificates	Remarks
Dorking					
Powell-Corderoy	Boys	60	12	4	7 Life Saving Certificates of the RLSS
	Girls	60	9	8	gained. 38 Certificates granted by the UDC
Church of England	Boys	30	8	8	
	Girls	28	8	7	
St Paul's C of E	Boys	30	10	13	Ten Life Saving Certificates gained
	Girls	31	8	14	
Westcott C of E	Boys	30	12	10	A long distance from the Bath
	Girls	34	10	6	
Coldharbour R.C.	Boys	11	6	0	This school's first swimming season
	Girls	11	6	0	One boy and 3 girls gained the Class IV Certificate given by the UDC
North Holmwood	Boys	14	3	1	This school's first swimming season
	Girls	12	2	1	A considerable distance from the Bath
Farnham					
West Street	Boys	40	17	19	The holders of many swimming trophies
St Polycarp's R.C.	Boys	17	1	0	This school was closed for over 5 weeks
	Girls	6	0	0	through sickness. The girls' first swimming lesson.
Hale	Boys	22	10	1	A long distance from the Bath.
Badshot Lea	Boys	40	16	4	" "
Bourne	Boys	13	3	2	" "
Wrecclesham	Boys	24	6	6	" "
Surbiton					
Christ Church	Boys	45	8	4	The number of attendances was considerably lessened owing to an epidemic of scarlet fever.
Hook, St Paul's	Boys	18	10	2	
	Girls	9	2	0	
St Andrew's Road, C of E	Boys	40	20	15	The girls first swimming season
	Girls	20	20	10	
Tolworth Council	Boys	31	30	17	A long distance from the Bath.
Tolworth, St Matthew's	Girls	30	13	1	" "
New Malden C of E	Boys	12	10	4	
Ham	Boys	26	10	5	The attendance was affected by
	Girls	14	5	1	scarlet fever
Long Ditton C of E	Boys	34	19	11	A long distance from the Bath
Sutton					
Benhilton C of E	Boys	32	23	11	
	Girls	15	8	1	
Crown Road Council	Boys	30	10	5	
	Girls	30	15	6	
New Town Council	Boys	54	15	12	
	Girls	29	15	3	
West Street Council	Boys	25	12	7	
Wallington					
Holy Trinity C of E	Boys	40	33	10	First swimming season. A long distance
	Girls	30	9	4	from the bath.

94

Beddington and	Boys	22	13	1	" "
Wallington C of E	Girls	16	9	0	

Merton & Mitcham

Merton C of E.	Boys	74	49	24	Challenge Cup won by J. Blythin. The insufficient accommodation at the Bath and the distance therefrom prevented the girls from taking swimming, but a number of them went, at their own expense out of school hours.
Lower Mitcham Council	Boys	47	8	6	First Swimming Season. The swimming took place in the River Wandle, no expense being incurred beyond provision of a dressing screen and lifebuoy. Of the six boys who have gained certificates, P. Jessup saved the life of W. Whiting whilst bathing during the holidays.

Horley

Lumley Road Council	Boys	60	16	7	Frank Honour, who learnt this season, saved the life of B. Humphery, who fell into the river.

Egham

Hythe Council	Boys	30	25	25	Winners of the Silver Challenge Shield
	Girls	20	7	6	The Staines Cup, for 100 yards championship was won by E. Oades. Girls first swimming season.
Station Road	Boys	40	17	11	The girls first swimming season. They were only able to attend six times, owing to wet weather and the long distance they had to go.

Walton

Walton-on-Thames Council	Boys	23	8	6	The school was closed in the middle of the course on account of an epidemic.
Oatlands Council	Boys	7	2	1	
	Girls	9	1	0	
Hersham Council	Boys	38	7	4	First swimming season.

Barnes & Mortlake

Barnes Westfields Council	Boys	71	17	6	" "
	Girls	19	10	1	
Mortlake Council	Boys	40	24	24	
	Girls	23	13	3	
Mortlake R.C.	Boys	26	8	3	First swimming season
	Girls	22	4	2	The fact that many of the children work from 6am until the school opens, coupled with the 2-mile walk to the Bath made regular attendance impossible. Several of the girls also could not pay for the necessary costume.

Godalming

Godalming C of E	Boys	40	25	12	No expense incurred by the SEC.

Shere

Holmbury St Mary's	Boys	20	4	0	" "
	Girls	18	4	0	
Frensham C of E	Boys	12	9	0	First swimming season. No expense incurred by the SEC

Guildford

Shalford Council	Boys	25	0	0	No expense incurred by the SEC
	Boys	1,351	552	310	
	Girls	568	194	75	
Totals		**1,919**	**746**	**385**	

Notes

1.   Appendix M.1, dd. 21 November 1909, pp.827-836 in *31st Report of the SEC* dd. 11 January 1910, 835.

APPENDIX XIV
SCHEDULE OF ESTIMATES FOR SWIMMING IN 1910[1]
(SURREY)

School	Department	Numbers	Total Tickets	£- s- d
DorkingDistrict				
Dorking, Powell Corderoy	Boys	40	960	4-00-00
	Girls	30	360	1-10-00
Dorking, C of E	Boys	40	960	4-00-00
	Girls	30	360	1-10-00
Dorking, St Paul's	Boys	40	480	2-00-00
	Girls	40	480	2-00-00
Dorking, Coldharbour RC	Boys	10	120	0-10-00
	Girls	10	120	0-10-00
Westcott C of E (Rural)	Boys	40	430	2-00-00
	Girls	30	360	1-10-00
North Holmwood	Boys	20	480	2-00-00
Farnham District				
Farnham, East Street Council	Boys	40	480	2-00-00
	Girls	20	240	1-00-00
West Street Council	Boys	40	480	2-00-00
St Polycarp's RC	Boys	20	480	2-00-00
	Girls	10	240	1-00-00
Hale Council (Rural)	Boys	20	240	1-00-00
Badshot Lea Council (Rural)	Boys	40	480	2-00-00
Bourne Council (Rural)	Boys	24	288	1-04-00
	Girls	12	144	12-00
Wrecclesham C of E (Rural)	Boys	20	240	1-00-00
Surbiton District				
Surbiton Hill, Christ Church	Boys	25	600	2-10-00
Surbiton, Hook St Paul's	Boys	20	240	1-00-00
	Girls	10	120	1-10-00
Surbiton, St Andrew's Road C of E	Boys	40	600	10-00
	Girls	20	400	1-13-04
Surbiton, Tolworth Council	Boys	30	720	3-00-00
Surbiton, Tolworth, St Matthews	Girls	30	300	3-15-00
New Malden, Council	Boys	20	240	1-00-00
	Girls	20	240	1-00-00
New Malden, C of E	Boys	20	360	1-10-00
Ham	Boys	36	360	1-10-00
	Girls	20	200	16-08
Long Ditton, C of E	Boys	40	480	2-00-00
Thames Ditton, Council	Boys	40	480	2-00-00
Sutton District				
Sutton, Benhilton C of E	Boys	30	360	1-10-00
	Girls	20	240	1-00-00
Sutton, Crown Road, C of E	Boys	30	360	1-10-00
	Girls	30	360	1-10-00

Sutton, New Town, Council	Boys	25	300	1-05-00
	Girls	25	300	1-05-00
Sutton, West Street, Council	Boys	25	300	1-05-00
Wallington, Holy Trinity, C of E	Boys	40	480	2-00-00
	Girls	40	480	2-00-00
Beddington & Wallington C of E	Boys	20	240	1-00-00
	Girls	10	120	10-00
Merton and Mitcham District				
Merton C of E	Boys	75	900	3-15-00
	Girls	25	300	1-05-00
Mitcham Singlegate	Boys	40	480	2-00-00
Mitcham, Lower Mitcham	Boys	50	1,000	4-03-04
Reigate District				
Merstham Council	Boys	20	280	2-06-08
Horley District				
Horley, Lumley Road, Council	Boys	60	60	1-10-00
Egham District				
Egham Hythe Council	Boys once a week	40 }		
	Girls twice a week	20 }		
Station Road Council	Boys once a week	40 }		6-06-00
	Girls once a week	24 }		
Walton District				
Walton-on-Thames Council	Boys	25 }		
	Girls	20 }		
Walton-on-Thames Oatlands Council	Boys	6 }		10-10-00
	Girls	6 }		
Barnes and Mortlake District				
Barnes, Westfield Council	Boys	40	480	4-00-00
	Girls	20	240	2-00-00
Barnes Green Council	Girls	20	240	2-00-00
Mortlake Council	Boys	40	480	4-00-00
	Girls	20	240	2-00-00
Mortlake RC	Boys	20	240	2-00-00
	Girls	20	240	2-00-00
				125-12-00
		Training of Teachers		10-00-00
		Apparatus		5-00-00
		Contingencies		9-08-00
				150-00-00

Additionally, swimming was to be taken by certain schools without any expense to the Committee unless possibly for apparatus or other small contingencies. The names of these and numbers of children attending would be given at the end of the season. A further five Woking schools were added as a result of the opening of the open air baths.

Note

1. Appendix MI dd. 22 March 1910 in *33rd Report of the SEC* dd. 10 May 1910.

APPENDIX XV
RESULTS OF THE 1910 SWIMMING SEASON (SURREY)

Source: Schedule B, Appendix E3 dd. 23 November 1910 in 36th Report of the SEC dd. 10 January 1911

School		Average Numbers Attending	Numbers Taught To Swim During Season	Numbers Who Gained County Certificates	Remarks
Dorking					
Powell Corderoy	Boys	30	18	7	5 boys and 4 girls obtained Life Saving Certificates.
	Girls	22	10	4	69 UDC certificates held by the school. 7 of those already holding County certificates swam over a mile this season.
Dorking C of E	Boys	32	16	6	Many UDC certificates obtained, also 2 for life saving
	Girls	26	14	11	
St Paul's C of E	Boys	40	20	7	18 UDC certificates gained by boys
	Girls	35	18	7	24 by the girls
Coldharbour RC	Boys	9	6	0	
	Girls	8	8	5	
Westcott C of E, Rural	Boys	19	4	3	A long distance from the bath.
	Girls	10	3	3	
North Holmwood, Rural	Boys	15	11	8	The girls' first swimming season. A long distance from the bath. Several UDC certificates gained.
	Girls	17	13	8	
Holmbury, St Mary's	Boys	16	4	4	No expense incurred by the SEC
	Girls	20	4	3	Swimming was taken in private water.
Farnham					
East Street Council	Boys	60	13	7	The holder of many swimming trophies
	Girls	45	4	0	
West Street Council	Boys	36	16	7	" " " "
Farnham C of E	Girls	29	29	0	This school's first swimming season
St Polycarps RC	Boys	19	9	5	
	Girls	10	4	0	
Hale, Rural	Boys	20	4	3	A long distance from the bath
Badshot Lea	Boys	50	18	0	" " "
Bourne Council	Boys	24	2	0	" " "
	Girls	12	0	0	" " "
Wrecclesham C of E	Boys	23	9	3	" " "
Frensham C of E	Boys	12	10	3	No expense incurred by the SEC Swimming taken in the light.
Surbiton					
Christ Church	Boys	50	20	9	
Hook, St Paul's	Boys	19	14	2	A long distance from the bath
	Girls	10	7	0	
St Andrew's Road	Boys	52	21	12	
C of E	Girls	30	16	7	
Tolworth Council	Boys	43	23	13	
Tolworth St Matthew's	Girls	23	6	2	
New Malden Council	Boys	20	16	10	This school's first swimming season
	Girls	12	5	2	A long distance from the bath
New Malden C of E	Boys	15	15	9	" " " "
Ham	Boys	26	6	1	
	Girls	20	10	4	

East Molesley C of E	Boys	19	7	3	This school's first swimming season. A long distance from the bath. Over and above the SEC's grant, £1-19-00 was paid by the Girls
	Girls	18	6	4	
Long Ditton C of E	Boys	39	16	6	
Thames Ditton Council	Boys	22	7	7	This school's first swimming season under the SEC. No expense incurred by the Committee. Swimmiing took place in private water.
Sutton					
Sutton, Benhilton C of E	Boys	30	20	12	
	Girls	20	12	4	
Crown Road Council	Boys	30	7	6	
	Girls	25	13	2	
New Town Council	Boys	25	15	5	
	Girls	25	17	4	
West street Council	Boys	25	10	5	
Belmont Council	Boys	25	10	1	No expense incurred by the SEC. Mr Bawtree paid all expenses
Wallington, Holy Trinity C of E	Boys	100	60	21	Excellent attendance, although a long way from the bath.
	Girls	30	24	6	
Beddington and Wallington C of E	Boys	0	0	0	This school did not take swimming although its distance from the bath was no greater than that of Holy Trinity.
	Girls	0	0	0	
Merton and Mitcham					
Merton C of E	Boys	72	34	18	The boys of this school won the Challenge Cup. The girls were refused the use of the Wimbledon Baths owing to insufficient room. Boys attendances excellent.
	Girls	0	0	0	
Merton, Raynes Park Council	Boys	23	11	0	This schools first swimming season. No expense incurred by the SEC in respect of the boys who paid for themselves.
	Girls	12	6	1	
Mitcham, Singlegate	Boys	50	40	20	This school's first swimming season. Attendance excellent. The boys and girls contributed to the attendance.
	Girls	15	8	4	
Lower Mitcham	Boys	29	7	7	No expense was incurred by the SEC Swimming taken in private water.
Reigate					
Merstham Council	Boys	20	13	11	This school's first swimming season. The boys paying their own railway fare to and from Reigate.
Horley					
Lumley Road Council	Boys	60	12	7	Excellent attendances. Mr Green's son, although not a teacher instructs the boys.
Egham					
Hythe Council	Boys	40	29	20	The boys of this school won the Staines Shield for the third year running.
	Girls	23	7	7	
Station Road Council	Boys	38	20	19	A long distance from the bathing place. The girls of this school only attended six times during the season owing to wet weather.
	Girls	24	6	0	
Woking					
Church Street Council	Boys	16	11	4	This school's first swimming season in the UDC new open air bath.
Goldsworth Road Council	Boys	29	9	9	" " " "
Maybury Council	Boys	31	11	7	" " " "
Monument Hill Council	Boys	24	12	9	" " " "
St John's Council	Boys	16	4	0	" " " "
Westfield Council	Boys	9	9	5	" " " "
Walton					
Walton-on-Thames Council	Boys	30	11	5	Swimming took place at the new UDC bathing place.
	Girls	20	3	2	
Walton-on-Thames Oatlands	Boys	11	1	1	" " "
Hersham	Boys	20	13	13	No expense incurred by SEC. Swimming took place in the River Mole. This school won the Inter-Schools Team Race.

Weybridge					
Weybridge C of E	Boys	15	14	13	No expense incurred by the SEC except for 5s 6d for six wings. First Swimming season. Swimming took place in the River Thames at the new UDC bathing place.
Barnes-Mortlake					
Barnes, Westfields	Boys	60	30	14	A long distance from the bath
Council	Girls	17	10	6	
Barnes Green	Girls	0	0	0	Did not take swimming
Barnes, Lonsdale Road	Boys	17	14	7	The school's first swimming season
					A long distance from the bath
Mortlake Council	Boys	47	29	16	A long distance from the bath
	Girls	20	15	10	
Mortlake RC	Boys	20	14	4	" " "
	Girls	20	9	0	
Godalming					
Godalming C of E	Boys	36	22	16	No expense incurred by the SEC
Guildford					
Shalford Council	Boys	50	0	0	" " "
					Only 3 lessons were taken owing to wet weather

Boys	1,688	809	411	
Girls	609	289	107	
Totals	**2,297***	**1,098****	**518**	

*   N. B. The total figures I calculate as 1708 boys, 598 girls=2306
**   The total figures I calculate as 831 boys, 253 girls=1084
(The actual numbers are, in a sense, not as important as the increase in the number of schools taking part year on year)
(The Superintendent's figures are quoted in all tables)

APPENDIX XVI
RESULTS OF THE 1911 SWIMMING SEASON (SURREY)
Source: Schedule B, Appendix E 2 dd 24 November 1911 in 41st Report of the SEC dd 9 January 1912.

School	Average Attendance		Numbers Taught To Swim	Numbers Gaining Certificates	Numbers Qualifying For Certificates	Remarks
Barnes-Mortlake						
Barnes, Lonsdale Road Council	Boys	28	15	12	3	Winners of the Challenge Shield, the first year of competition
Barnes, Westfields Council	Boys	60	26	8	7	All the schools in this district are a long way from the bath.
	Girls	15	7	-	1	
Mortlake Council	Boys	33	20	11	8	The swimming sports held at the close of the season were excellent. Thanks to the efforts of the headteachers great interest was taken in them. Many prizes were presented by the outside public. *
	Girls	17	9	2	2	
Mortlake RC	Boys	14	7	2	-	
	Girls	13	4	-	-	
Dorking						
Dorking C of E	Boys	29	12	9	3	Many UDC and Life Saving certificates were gained by the schools in this district. The annual swimming sports were excellent. One girl swam 1¼ miles.
	Girls	18	6	5	7	
St Paul's C of E	Boys	24	9	5	10	
	Girls	28	7	5	8	
Coldharbour RC	Boys	6	2	-	-	
	Girls	10	3	2	3	
North Holmwood C of E Rural	Boys	14	5	2	4	A long distance from the bath
	Girls	12	6	3	5	
Westcott C of E Rural	Boys	16	7	2	1	
	Girls	9	2	1	1	" " "
Shere, Holmbury, St Mary's C of E	Boys	8	2	2	3	No expense incurred by the SEC. Swimming takes place in private water.
	Girls	6	4	5	2	
Egham						
Hythe Council	Boys	40	29	21	7	The Silver Challenge Shield for Staines and District was won by the school for the fourth year. The Challenge Cup for the year was won by Alfred Tyler.
	Girls	20	5	2	2	
Station Road Council	Boys	36	14	13	11	A long distance from the bathing place.
	Girls	18	5	-	-	
Farnham						
East Street Council	Boys	48	16	9	8	The holder of many swimming trophies.
	Girls	26	5	1	-	
West Street Council	Boys	25	19	9	6	" " "
Farnham C of E	Girls	18	-	-	-	Only able to take the Course this season.
St Polycarp's RC	Boys	17	7	5	-	
	Girls	10	4	-	-	
Badshot Lea Council (Rural)	Boys	20	20	11	-	A long distance from the bath
Bourne Council (Rural)	Boys	24	8	4	2	" " "
	Girls	9	-	-	-	
Hale (Rural)	Boys	19	5	2	-	" " "
Wrecclesham (Rural)	Boys	17	9	8	2	" " "

School						Notes
Frensham C of E	Boys	14	5	7	1	No expense incurred by the SEC. Swimming was taken in the lake. 6 out of the 7 boys who gained certificates also qualified in Life Saving.
Godalming						
Godalming C of E	Boys	35	20	18	6	No expense incurred by the SEC }
Godalming Council	Boys	21	17	14	-	Through the courtesy of Charterhouse }
Farncombe C of E	Boys	44	27	23	-	swimming was taken in their bathing }
Busbridge C of E (Rural)	Boys	14	10	1	-	place. This was the first season of } Godalming Council,and Farncombe and Busbridge. }
Guildford						
Shalford Council	Boys	80	27	13	-	No expense incurred by the SEC.
Horley						
Lumley Road Council	Boys	37	20	12	4	Mr Green's son, although not a teacher, instructs the boys.
Merton & Mitcham						
Merton C of E	Boys	67	67	32	9	Excellent results. Winner of Challenge Cup Cecil Sheppard
	Girls	18	7	5	-	
Merton, Raynes Park Council	Boys	27	15	11	1	The girls were unable to attend owing to insufficient room at Wimbledon Bath.
	Girls	-	-	-	-	
Mitcham, Lower Mitcham Council	Boys	41	14	9	3	No expense incurred by the SEC. Swimming was taken in private water.
Mitcham, Singlegate Council	Boys	46	27	11	10	One boy won 100 yards Championship (open to boys of Wimbledon, Merton and Mitcham). 2 boys swam over a mile and 2 others over ¾ of a mile.
	Girls	14	13	3	-	
Reigate						
Merstham Council	Boys	20	16	8	3	The boys paid their own railway fare to and from Reigate
Surbiton						
Christ Church	Boys	42	14	5	1	
Hook, St Paul's	Boys	9	9	4	1	A long distance from the bath.
	Girls	3	3	1	-	
St Andrew's Road C of E	Boys	48	20	10	11	
	Girls	24	7	4	7	
Tolworth Council	Boys	50	25	12	7	
Tolworth, St Matthew's	Girls	25	12	3	1	
New Malden, C of E	Boys	22	10	8	2	A long distance from the bath.
New Malden East Council	Boys	24	6	1	2	" " "
Ham C of E	Boys	14	7	3	1	
	Girls	21	9	5	2	
East Molesley C of E	Boys	30	30	30	1	Excellent results. A number of the boys paid for extra tickets. An 'old boy' presented a 'learners' prize. A long distance from the bath.
	Girls	14	4	3	-	
Long Ditton C of E	Boys	33	12	9	7	A long distance from the bath.
Thames Ditton Council	Boys	20	4	13	2	No expense incurred by the SEC. Swimming was taken in private water.
Sutton						
Belmont Council	Boys	26	18	1	-	No expense incurred by the SEC. Mr Bawtree paid all expenses.
Benhilton C of E	Boys	25	13	5	7	
	Girls	15	-	-	1	
Crown Road Council	Boys	30	22	10	1	
	Girls	25	14	5	3	
New Town Council	Boys	25	9	3	3	This school won the Girls' Challenge Shield for the district, this being the first year of competition.
	Girls	25	15	6	-	
West Street Council	Boys	25	14	8	2	
Wallington, Holy Trinity C of E	Boys	75	32	7	12	This school won the Boys' Challenge Shield for the district, the first year of the competetion. A long distance from the bath.
	Girls	20	15	2	2	

School						Notes
Beddington and Wallington C of E	Boys	23	13	2	-	This school's first swimming season. A long distance from the bath.
	Girls	11	3	-	-	
Carshalton RC	Boys	9	4	4	-	This school's first swimming season. A long distance from the bath.
	Girls	9	-	-	-	
Walton-on-Thames						
Walton-on-Thames Council	Boys	25	14	15	5	
	Girls	15	7	5	-	
Oatlands Council	Boys	7	4	1	-	The girls did not begin attendance until 11 July owing to no notification from correspondent.
	Girls	9	-	-	-	
Hersham Council	Boys	19	16	11	6	No expense incurred by the SEC. Swimming taken in the River Mole.
Weybridge						
Weybridge C of E.	Boys	25	22	12	-	No expense incurred by the SEC. Swimming took place in the River Thames at the new UDC Bathing place.
Windlesham						
Bagshot	Boys	6	6	3	-	This school's first swimming season.
Woking						
Church Street Council	Boys	16	15	9	4	This was the Girls' first swimming season, last year being the first in the district when only the boys attended. The results of some of the latter were most encouraging.
	Girls	13	-	-	-	
Goldsworth Road Council	Boys	34	16	10	4	
	Girls	21	1	-	-	
Maybury Council	Boys	31	20	17	-	
	Girls	14	-	-	-	
Monument Hill Council	Boys	24	14	9	5	The girls could not attend as no mistress could swim.
	Girls	-	-	-	-	
St John's Council	Boys	16	5	1	-	" " "
	Girls	-	-	-	-	
Westfield Council	Boys	25	22	10	-	
	Girls	17	1	-	-	
Knaphill	Boys	16	4	-	-	The first season for which boys and girls. A long distance from the Bath.
	Girls	11	-	-	-	
	Boys	1,722	931	539	200	
	Girls	588	194	78	50	
Totals		**2,310**	**1,125**	**617**	**250**	

*   The Superintendent later acknowledged that these swimming sports were the Westfield Swimming Sports at which Burgess the Channel Swimmer gave an exhibition.

Note: The Burgess referred to by the Superintendent was TW Burgess who swam the Channel from Dover to Cape Gris Nez in 2 hrs 35 mins September 5th-6th 1911. This was his 16th attempt.

APPENDIX XVII
RESULTS OF SWIMMING IN 1913 (SURREY)

Source: Appendix E 2 dd 28 November 1913 in 51st Report of the SEC dd 13 January 1914

School		Average Attendance	Numbers Taught To To Swim Exclusive Of Those Who Gained Certificates	Numbers Gaining Certificates	Numbers Qualifying For Endorsement	Remarks
Barnes-Mortlake						
Barnes Green,	Girls	16	6	-	-	All the schools in this district were a long way from the Bath.
Barnes, Lonsdale, Road Council	Boys	33	12	7	9	
Barnes, Westfields Council	Boys	60	8	12	9	The Westfields Swimming Gala, held
	Girls	14	9	2	-	at the close of the season was excellent
Mortlake Council	Boys	60	13	27	13	The boys won the Westfields Challenge
	Girls	60	21	15	6	Shield; also the Mortlake Championship Gold Medal. They also gained 20 First Class London Schools' Swimming Association Certificates; and the girls gained 16.
Mortlake C of E	Boys	76	21	27	-	This school's first swimming season
	Girls	74	13	6	-	under the SEC. No expense incurred by the SEC. Two boys each swam over a mile.
Mortlake R.C.	Boys	18	5	2	1	One of the boys swam over ¾ mile.
	Girls	12	2	-	-	
Dorking						
Dorking C of E	Boys	30	7	13	6	The girls again won the Maurice
	Girls	22	4	12	6	Challenge Cup. One girl swam 2¼ miles another 2 miles, three over 1½ miles, and five others a mile each.
Coldharbour R.C.	Boys	11	2	6	3	One boy swam ¾ mile
	Girls	12	-	8	4	
Powell-Corderoy	Boys	24	6	10	4	Forty-one UDC Certificates obtained.
	Girls	23	6	4	8	One pupil swam 2½ miles, two each 1¾ miles, three 1½ miles and four 1 mile.
St Paul's C of E	Boys	28	2	15	5	The Boys' District Challenge Cup was
	Girls	31	-	21	7	won by this school for the 5th year in succession. One girl swam 2 miles, three girls and two boys each swam a mile.
(Rural) North Holmwood	Boys	14	3	4	7	Thirteen UDC certificates obtained. A long distance from the Bath.
(Rural) Westcott C of E	Boys	11	3	6	2	One girl swam over ¾ mile. A long
	Girls	11	6	3	-	distance from the Bath.
Shere, Holmbury	Boys	13	7	2	3	No expense incurred by the SEC.
St Mary's	Girls	16	5	1	3	Swimming taken in private water.
Egham, Hythe Council	Boys	39	10	10	7	This makes the 5th year in which the boys
	Girls	20	5	3	-	have won the Staines District Silver Sheild also the Open Championship Silver Cup.

School						Notes
Egham, Station Road Council	Boys	40	5	13	5	Walter Franks rescued Wellwood Gardener from drowning in the Thames on August 20th . Four of the girls almost succeeded in getting certificates.
	Girls	20	12	-	-	
Epsom						
Epsom, C of E	Boys	9	5	4	-	This school's first swimming season. No expense incurred by the SEC.
Farnham						
Farnham C of E	Girls	18	4	-	-	
East Street Council	Boys	37	15	8	4	Winners of Shield and Inter-Schools Championship; also other trophies.
	Girls	30	5	3	1	
West Street Council	Boys	25	13	3	7	This school also holds many swimming trophies.
St Polycarp's RC	Boys	13	2	1	5	
	Girls	12	-	-	-	
(Rural) Badshot Lea Council	Boys	21	3	2	1	A long distance from the Bath.
(Rural) Bourne	Boys	19	1	2	-	" " "
	Girls	7	1	-	-	" " "
(Rural) Hale Council	Boys	33	6	-	-	" " "
(Rural) Wrecclesham C of E	Boys	16	3	-	1	" " "
Frensham C of E	Boys	26	10	16	-	No expense incurred by the SEC
Godalming						
Godalming C of E	Boys	35	12	10	5	" " "
Godalming Council	Boys	18	5	12	4	" " "
Farncombe C of E	Boys	45	5	9	5	" " "
(Rural) Busbridge C of E	Boys	14	7	3	1	" " "
Elstead C of E	Boys	10	1	2	-	This school's first swimming season.
Thursley C of E	Boys	10	4	-	-	" " "
Guildford						
East Clandon C of E	Boys	-	-	-	-	Unable to attend this year
Shalford Council	Boys	40	6	3	6	No expense incurred by the SEC
Shere C of E	Boys	16	1	2	-	" " "
	Girls	17	2	4	-	This school's first swimming season
Wonersh and Shamley Green C of E	Boys	12	3	-	-	This school's first swimming season. No expense incurred by the SEC. Mr Rawnsley very kindly built a bathing place for the children.
Horley						
Albert Road Council	Girls	18	-	-	-	This school's first swimming season
Lumley Road Council	Boys	25	9	2	3	
Merton & Mitcham						
Merton C of E	Boys	60	18	23	10	The Merton Schools Championship Cup was won by Albert Brown.
	Girls	20	7	8	3	
Merton, Raynes Park Council	Boys	52	20	16	4	The boys and girls contributed to the cost of the tickets
	Girls	26	-	1	-	
Merton, Aston Road Council	Boys	17	7	-	-	This school's first swimming season. The children contributed towards the cost of tickets.
	Girls	17	3	-	-	
Mitcham, Fortescue Road, Council	Boys	38	6	8	2	The two boys who got endorsements swam a mile this year.
	Girls	18	16	5	-	
Mitcham, Links Council	Boys	-	-	-	-	Unable to attend
	Girls	-	-	-	-	
Mitcham, Lower Mitcham Council	Boys	38	8	11	4	No expense incurred by the SEC
Mitcham, Singlegate Council	Boys	62	8	13	13	Three boys each swam 1 mile and 6 half a mile. The boys won the District Team Race. The girls won the Team Race for girls under 13. 3 girls each swam a mile.
	Girls	48	19	7	3	
Reigate						
Chipstead Council	Boys	9	2	2	-	This school's first swimming season for County Certificates. All expenses are paid by the Mary Stephen's Endowment Fund.

Merstham Council	Boys	21	8	8	-	The boys paid their own railway fares to and from Reigate.
Ripley						
	Boys	26	13	4	-	This school's first swimming season.
	Girls	30	2	-	-	
Surbiton						
Christ Church C of E	Boys	27	3	1	-	
	Girls	22	8	3	1	
Hook St Paul's C of E	Boys	10	4	5	1	A long distance from the Bath.
	Girls	10	3	3	1	
St Andrew's Road C of E	Boys	31	6	5	9	Canon Potter kindly presented 2 cups, one for the boys and one for the girls, to be competed for each year. Two boys each swam just upon 2 miles.
	Girls	20	10	8	1	
Tolworth Council	Boys	30	8	12	7	
Tolworth St Matthew's C of E	Girls	17	10	3	1	
New Malden C of E	Boys	19	9	4	3	Runners up in the Inter-Schools Competition. A long distance from the bath.
	Girls	16	4	-	-	
New Malden East Council	Boys	-	-	-	-	Owing to shortage of staff, distance from the Baths and inconvenient times, this school was unfortunately unable to take swimming this year.
	Girls	-	-	-	-	
New Malden West, Council	Boys	9	1	3	2	A long distance from the Bath.
Ham C of E	Boys	13	4	-	3	" " "
	Girls	17	4	3	1	
East Molesey C of E	Boys	20	-	5	1	" " "
Long Ditton C of E	Boys	26	5	4	3	" " "
	Girls	24	5	-	-	
Thames Ditton Council	Boys	12	2	4	-	No expense incurred by the SEC.
Sutton						
Belmont Council	Boys	26	8	4	-	
	Girls	20	4	-	-	The Girls' first swimming season.
Benhilton C of E	Boys	27	8	9	4	One boy won the Sutton Swimming and Diving Championship, also the Junior Championships of London and the Southern Counties. The girls won the Sutton Junior Championship.
	Girls	18	7	2	-	
Crown Road Council	Boys	24	7	9	2	Runners-up in the Inter-Schools Team Championship races. Two of the boys swam nearly ¾ of a mile. The girls won the District Championship and Shield for the girls.
	Girls	26	13	2	2	
New Town Council	Boys	36	13	14	5	The boys won the District Championship and shield for boys.
	Girls	25	13	5	2	
West Street Council	Boys	25	5	6	4	
Wallington, Bandon Hill Council	Boys	45	21	10	-	This school's first swimming season. The children trammed to the Baths, 3 miles from the school, and paid their own fares.
	Girls	20	2	-	-	
Hackbridge Council	Boys	28	18	4	1	Frederick Bates won the medal for Life-Saving, given by Mrs Aitken. A long distance from the Bath.
Holy Trinity C of E	Boys	57	15	13	2	A long distance from the Bath.
	Girls	24	8	8	8	
Beddington and Wallington C of E	Boys	24	5	8	5	Of the 5 boys who received endorsements, three swam 1000 yards each and the remaining two ¾ of a mile. Doris Williams won the 50 yards Championship. A long distance from the Bath.
	Girls	18	8	4	2	

Carshalton, St Mary's RC	Boys	16	4	2	7	William Jenner and George Hills saved a boy from drowning. For this they received the Sutton Special Certificate for Life-saving. A long distance from the Bath.
	Girls	12	5	1	2	
Carshalton, Stanley Road Council	Boys	16	1	1	-	A long distance from the Bath.
	Girls	12	-	-	-	
Walton-On-Thames						
Walton-on-Thames Council	Boys	20	1	17	-	The boys won the Inter-Schools Race and Medals.
	Girls	14	5	2	4	
Oatlands Council	Boys	8	2	2	5	
	Girls	7	3	2	-	
Hersham Council	Boys	15	4	5	-	No expense incurred by the SEC.
Weybridge						
Weybridge C of E	Boys	30	7	11	13	No expense incurred by the SEC. One boy swam 1 mile, two ¾ of a mile and one ½ a mile. The "Stern" Challenge Cup became the property of the School last year.
	Girls	34	10	10	-	
Windlesham						
Bagshot, Council	Boys	18	11	3	1	
Woking						
Brookwood Council	Boys	11	2	1	-	This school's first swimming season.
Church Street Council	Boys	18	7	7	3	
	Girls	14	7	-	-	
Goldsworth Road Council	Boys	22	4	4	2	Two of the boys swam over ½ a mile.
	Girls	20	-	2	-	
Knaphill Council	Boys	17	6	-	-	Nearly all Woking Schools are a long distance from the Bath.
	Girls	12	3	-	-	
Maybury Council	Boys	28	6	10	2	
	Girls	10	-	-	-	
Monument Hill Council	Boys	28	9	6	6	
St John's Council	Boys	18	-	-	-	
	Girls	7	-	-	-	The Girls' first swimming season.
Westfield Council	Boys	17	2	7	3	
	Girls	20	2	2	-	
	Boys	1,895	491	504	239	
	Girls	998	273	163	63	
Totals		**2,893**	**764**	**667**	**302**	

APPENDIX XVIII
THE DEVELOPMENT OF SWIMMING IN SURREY'S ELEMENTARY SCHOOLS 1907-1922

Year	Schools	Departments Participating			Children Under Instruction			Children Learning To Swim			Certificates Awarded			E
		Boys	Girls	Total	Boys	Girls	Total	Boys	Girls	Total	Boys	Girls	Total	
1907	29	29	9	39				342	61	403				
1908	35	34	12	46	978	254	1,232	430	92	522				
1909	42	41	26	67	1,351	568	1,919	552	194	746	310	75	385	
1910	57	55	30	85	1,688	609	2,297	809	289	1,098	411	107	518	
1911	65	62	37	99	1,722	588	2,310	931	194	1,125	539	78	617	250
1913	80	76	52	128	1,895	998	2,893	491	273	764	504	163	667	B.239 G. 63
1917	29			47	716	450	1,166			636			301	107
1918	44			68	998	672	1,670	348	207	555			341	154
1922	93	90	70	160			3,730			998			736	

E = Certificates Endorsed

Sources: *Statistics collated from SEC Reports commencing 22nd Report of the SEC dd 11 February 1908 & ending with 95th Report of the SEC dd 13 March 1923.*

BIBLIOGRAPHY

The National Archives

Ed. 19/7	Borough of New Windsor Letter
Ed. 19/192	Northamptonshire County Council Letter
Ed. 19/192	Board of Education Letter
Ed. 21/16856b	Stepgates School Chertsey
Ed. 21/16882	British School Dorking
Ed. 21/16896	Egham Hythe School Staines
Ed. 21/16897	St Ann's School, Virginia Water
Ed. 21/16898	Egham School, Egham (Manorcroft)
Ed. 21/16934	Godalming National School
Ed. 21/17053	Goldsworth School, Woking
Ed. 111/117	Northamptonshire County Council Letter
Ed. 111/126	Borough of Newark Education Committee
Ed. 111/213	County Borough of Hastings
Ed. 125/21	Cornwall Education Committee
Ed. 125/21	Yorkshire West Riding
Ed. 125/21	Cheshire County Council Letter
Ed. 125/21	Board of Education Letter

Acts of Parliament

The Elementary Education Act, 1870
33 and 34 Victoria, Chapter 75

Elementary Education Act, 1873
36 and 37 Victoria, Chapter 86

The Public Health Act, 1875
38 & 39 Victoria, Chapter 55
(incorporating The Baths and Washhouses Act, 1846-9 & 10 Victoria, Chapter 74)

The Elementary Education Act, 1876
39 and 40 Victoria, Chapter 79

Board of Education Act, 1899
62 and 63 Victoria, Chapter 33

The Education Act, 1902
2 Edward 7, Chapter 42

The Education (London) Act, 1903
3 Edward 7, Chapter 24

Education (Provision of Meals) Act, 1906
6 Edward VII, Chapter 57

Local Education Authorities, (Medical Treatment) Act, 1909
9 Edward VII, Chapter 13

Education (Provision of Meals) Act, 1914
4 & 5 Geo V, Chapter 20

Education Act, 1918
8 and 9 George V, Chapter 39

Education Act, 1921
1 and 12 George 5, Chapter 51

Parliamentary Papers

PP XXV, 1886; PP XXIX + XXX, 1887; PP XXXv-XXXVII, 1888;
Reports of the Royal Commission to enquire into the working of the Elementary Education Acts, 1886-
    1888.
PP Volume XXX, 1, Command 1507, *Report of the Royal Commission on Physical Training (Scotland),*
    Volume 1 Report and Appendix, 1903.
PP Volume XXX, Command 1508, *Report of the Royal Commission on Physical Training (Scotland),*
    Volume II Minutes of Evidence and Index, 1903.
PP Volume XXXII, Command 2175, *Report of the Inter-Departmental Committee on Physical
    Deterioration,* Volume I Report and Appendix, 1904.
PP Volume XXXII, Command 2210, *Minutes of Evidence taken before the Inter-Departmental Committee
    on Physical Deterioration*, Volume II List of Witnesses and Minutes of Evidence, 1904.
PP Volume XIX, Command 2032, *Report of the Inter-Departmental Committee on the Model Course of
    Physical Exercises*, 1904.

Thesis

Pegg, John Robert, *The Impact of Contemporary and Historical Influences on Aspects of Physical
    Education in Elementary Schools in Surrey 1894-1930.* Dissertation submitted in partial
    fulfillment of the requirements for the degree of Master of Arts (Education) at King's College,
    University of London, 1985. (A copy is deposited at the SHC Woking)

Log Books

Egham Hythe Boys' School (Commenced 15 March 1886)
Egham Hythe Girls' School (Commenced 15 March 1886)
Godalming National Boys' School (Commenced 1 May 1883: Closed 29 May 1914)
Godalming National Boys' School (Commenced 9 June 1914)

Surrey History Centre

C/EM/67/1-4	Egham School Minutes, 23 April 1907 to 23 July 1929
C/ES/115	Dorking British (Powell-Corderoy) School Records
C/ES/115/1/1/1-4	Minute Books 1873-1911
C/ES/115/1/6/10	Address to the School on the Institution of the Charlie Warner Swimming Prize
C/ES/115/2/1/1	Log Book 1889-1919

C/ES/115/2/1/2   Log Book 1920-1950
C/ES/115/2/4/21   Scholars Magazine
C/ES/115/2/4/44   Honours Lists

Surrey Education Committee Reports

13th Report of the SEC,	13 February 1906.
17th Report of the SEC,	13 November 1906.
19th Report of the SEC,	14 May 1907.
22nd Report of the SEC,	11 February 1908.
23rd Report of the SEC,	12 May 1908.
24th Report of the SEC,	28 July 1908.
25th Report of the SEC,	10 November 1908.
27th Report of the SEC,	16 March 1909.
28th Report of the SEC,	11 May 1909.
31st Report of the SEC,	11 January 1910.
32nd Report of the SEC,	15 March 1910.
33rd Report of the SEC,	10 May 1910.
34th Report of the SEC,	26 July 1910.
36th Report of the SEC,	10 January 1911.
37th Report of the SEC,	14 March 1911.
38th Report of the SEC,	9 May 1911.
39th Report of the SEC,	25 July 1911.
41st Report of the SEC,	9 January 1912.
42nd Report of the SEC,	12 March 1912.
51st Report of the SEC,	13 January 1914.
66th Report of the SEC,	31st July 1917.
71st Report of the SEC,	12 March 1918.
75th Report of the SEC,	11 March 1919.
82nd Report of the SEC,	27 July 1920.
95th Report of the SEC,	13 March 1923.

Newspapers

School Board Chronicle (26-10-1889)
The Dorking Journal
The Dorking and Leatherhead Advertiser
The (Hull) Daily Mail
The Schoolmaster
The Surrey Herald
The Surrey Times
The Sutton Advertiser
The Woking Observer
West Middlesex Times

Board of Education

Code of Regulations for Day Schools with Schedules and Appendices 1907
Syllabus of Physical Exercises for use in Public Elementary Schools 1904
Syllabus of Physical Exercises for use in Public Elementary Schools 1905
The Syllabus of Physical Exercises for Public Elementary Schools 1909
Syllabus of Physical Training for Schools 1919

Education Department

Code of Regulations for Day Schools with Schedules and Appendices 1894-1901

London Metropolitan Archives
School Board for London

SBL 22.66 Report of the Physical Education Sub-Committee on Bathing Accommodation and Swimming Classes (Public Elementary Schools) with Appendices pp.1-41. May 1890.

SBL 22.66 School Management Sub-Committee, Special Subjects Sub-Committee, School Board for London, Supplement to Swimming Return for the year ended Lady Day 1903. (Lady Day = 25 March)

SBL 22.66 Appendix A, Report submitted to the London School Board by the Works Committee on 26 June 1872 reprinted in the May 1890 Report.

Hansard

Hansard, Volume 107, 4th Series, 5 May 1902.
Hansard, Volume 140, 4th Series, 11 August 1904.

Secondary Sources

Alexander, Michael. A verse translation, *Beowulf.* Penguin Books, Harmondsworth, Middlesex, 1973.

Aries, Philippe. *Centuries of Childhood, 1960.* Peregrine Edition, Harmondsworth, Middlesex, 1979.

Austin, H R. *How To Swim.* Methuen & Co Ltd, London, 1914.

Ayriss, Chris. *Hung Out To Dry, Swimming and British Culture.* www.Lulu.com, 2011.

Barlow, Sir Montague and Holland, Richard. *The Education Act, 1918.* National Society Depository, London, 1918.

Bibbero, Marquis, Professor. *Athletics and Physical Training (For Land and Water).* Walbrook & Co Ltd., London, 1901.

Bingham, J H Alderman, JP. *The Period of the Sheffield School Board 1870-1903.* J W Northend Limited, Sheffield, 1949.

Cates, Joseph. *The Welfare of the School Child.* Cassell and Company, Ltd, London, 1919.

Clias, Captain P H. *An Elementary Course of Gymnastic Exercises Intended To develop and Improve The Physical Powers of Man with The Report made to the Medical Faculty of Paris on the Subject and a New and Complete Treatise on the Art of Swimming.* Printed for Sherwood, Gilbert and Piper, Fourth Edition, London, 1825.

Dalton, Frank Eugen. *Swimming Scientifically Taught.* Funk & Wagnalls Company, New York, 1912. A Kessinger Legacy Reprint

Dierden, Margaret and Barrett, Jane. *Shalford School, 150 years of a Village School 1885-2005.* Shalford Infant School, Shalford, Surrey, GU4 8BY, 2005.

Digby Everard. *De Are Natandi Libri Duo Quorum Prior Regulus Ipsius Artis, Posterior Vero Praxin Demonstrationemque Continet. Authore Everardo Dygbeio Anglo In Artibus Magistro.* Excudebat Thomas Dawson, 1587, EEBO Edition

Drury, J F W. *Drury's Manual of Education.* John Heywood, 1903.

Dukes, Clement. *Health at School.* New and Enlarged Edition, Cassell & Company Limited, London, 1887.

Dukes, Clement. *Health At School.* Third Edition, Revised, Enlarged and Illustrated. Rivington, Percival & Co., London, 1894.

Elyot, Sir Thomas. *The Governour, 1531.* Everyman's Library, J M Dent & Sons Ltd, London, 1907.

Freeman, Kenneth J., Randall, M J. Edited. *Schools of Hellas, An Essay On The Theory and Practice of Ancient Greek Education from 600 to 300BC.* Third Edition, MacMillan & Co Ltd, London, 1922.

Grant, Ruth W. and Tarcov Nathan, Edited. Locke, John. *Some Thoughts Concerning Education (1693) and Of the Conduct of the Understanding, (1706).* Hackett Publishing Company, Inc., Indianapolis, Indiana, 1996.

GutsMuths, Johann Christoph Friedrich. *Gymnastics for Youth: Or A Practical Guide To Healthful and Amusing Exercises For The Use of Schools. An Essay Toward the Necessary Improvement of Education, Chiefly As It Relates to the Body.* J Johnson, London, 1800.

Hodder, Thomas Knowles. Edited. *Daily Express Book of Popular Sports.* Daily Express Publications, London, (nd) (1935?)

Holbein, Montague A. *Swimming.* C Arthur Pearson Ltd., London, 1903.

Hutt, C W. *Crowley's Hygiene of School Life.* Methuen & Co Ltd, Sixth Edition, London, 1924.

Jessop, Gilbert & Salmand J B. Editors. *The Book of School Sports.* Thomas Nelson & Sons Ltd, London, (nd).

Juvenal. Green, Peter, translated. *The Sixteen Satires.* Penguin, Harmondsworth, 1967.

Kerr, James and Wallis, E White, Edited. *Second International Congress on School Hygiene.* Volumes I, II and III, The Royal Sanitary Institute, London, 1907.

Locke, John. Grant, Ruth W & Tarcov, Nathan, Edited. *Some Thoughts Concerning Education and Of the Conduct of the Understanding,* Hackett Publishing Co Inc., Indianapolis, Indiana, 1996.

Lyte, Sir H C Maxwell, KCB. *A History of Eton College (1440-1898).* Third Edition, MacMillan & Co Ltd, London, 1899.

McIntosh, Peter C. *Physical Education in England Since 1800.* Revised & Enlarged Edition, London, 1968.

Macaulay, Thomas Babington. *Lays of Ancient Rome & miscellaneous essays and poems.* Everyman's Library, Dent, 1910.

Marlowe, Christopher, Gill, Roma, Edited. *The Complete Works of Christopher Marlowe.* Clarendon Press, Oxford, 1987.

May, Jonathan. *Madame Bergman-Osterberg, Pioneer of Physical Education and Games for Girls and Women.* George G Harrap & Co Ltd, London, 1969.

Moss, Peter. *Sports and Pastimes Through the Ages.* George G Harrap & Co Ltd, London, 1962.

Mulcaster, Richard. *Positions.* With an Appendix, containing some account of his life and writings by Quick, Robert Herbert, Longmans, Green and Co., London, 1888.

Mulcaster, Richard. DeMolen Richard L, Abridged and Edited. *Richard Mulcaster's Positions.* Teachers College Press, Columbia University, New York, 1971.

Oliphant, James. *The Educational Writings of Richard Mulcaster (1532-1611).* James Maclehose and Sons, Glasgow, 1903.

Orme, Nicholas. *Early British Swimming 55BC-AD1719.* University of Exeter, 1983.

Orme, Nicholas. *Medieval Children.* Yale University Press, New Haven, Paperback Edition, 2003.

Parr, Susie. *The Story of Swimming, A Social History of Bathing in Britain.* Dewi Lewis Media, Heaton Moor, Stockport, 2011.

Peacham, Henry and Gordon G S. *Peacham's Compleat Gentlemen.* 1634, Clarendon Press, Oxford, 1906.

Pegg, J Robert, *Quick March! To Athletic Sports, The Origins and Development of Drill, Athletics, Cricket, Football and Swimming in Croydon's Public Elementary Schools 1893-1910: A Newspaper, Documentary History.* Angela Blaydon Publishing Limited, Ripley, Surrey, 2011.

Plato. Hamilton, Walter translated. *Phaedrus and The Seventh and Eighth Letters.* Penguin Books, Harmondsworth, Middlesex, 1973.

Plato, *The Republic.* Lee H D P translated, Penguin Books, Harmondsworth, Midddlesex, 1955.

Plato, *The Laws.* Trevor J Saunders translated, Penguin Books, Harmondsworth, 1970.

Rousseau, Jean-Jacques. *Emile.* translated by Barbara Foxley, Paperback Edition Everyman's Library, J M Dent & Sons Ltd, London, 1974.

Sachs, Frank. *The Complete Swimmer.* Methuen & Co Ltd., London, 1912.

Seaborne, Malcolm and Lowe, Roy. *The English School, Its Architecture and Organization.* Volume II 1870-1970, Routledge & Kegan Paul, London, 1977.

Sinclair, Archibald and Henry, William. *Swimming*. 2nd Edition, Longmans Green & Co., London, 1894.

Smith, Ann Avery. *Swimming and Plain Diving*. Charles Scribner's Sons, London, 1930.

Spalding, Thomas Alfred and Canney, Thomas Stanley Alfred. *The Work of the London School Board*. Second Edition Revised, P S King & Son, London.

Swaddling, Judith. *The Ancient Olympic Games*. Third Edition, The British Museum Press, London, 2004.

The Amateur Swimming Association. *Swimming and Swimming Strokes*. (1935 Revised), Simpkin Marshall Ltd, London, 1943.

Thompson, Della. Edited. *The Oxford Compact English Dictionary*. OUP, 1996.

Tissot, J-C. *Medicinal & Surgical Gymnastics or Essay On the Usefulness of Movement, or different Exercises of the body, & of rest, in the treatment of Diseases*. Bastien, Paris, 1780. Translated by Elizabeth and Sidney Licht, 1964, Elizabeth Licht, New Haven, Connecticut, 1964.

Walker, Donald. *British Manly Exercises*. T Hurst, London, 1834.

Welpton, W P. *Principles and Methods of Physical Education and Hygiene*. University Tutorial Press Ltd, 1912.

Wilson, William. *The Swimming Instructor, A Treatise on the Art of Swimming and Diving*. Horace Cox, London, 1883.

Wolffe, Jappy. *The Text Book of Swimming*. Ewart, Seymour & Co Ltd, London, 1908(?).